The Headshot Handbook

A Step-by-Step Guide to Headshot Photography

AMANDA OTIS

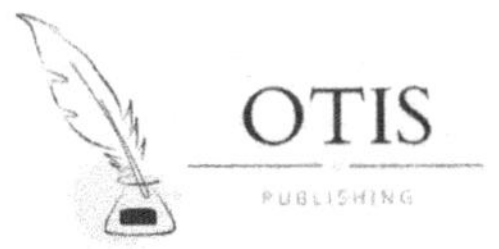

OTIS
PUBLISHING

Contents

Introduction

There was once a young actor who, after countless auditions and minimal callbacks, decided on a whim to update his headshot. He opted for a photographer who believed in capturing both faces and stories. The result? A headshot that didn't just showcase his features but his enthusiasm and spirit. Within weeks, his new headshot swung open doors that seemed previously bolted shut—leading to pivotal roles and a transformative boost in confidence. This isn't just any story; it's a testament to the power of a single photo.

My journey into the world of headshot photography began at the crossroads of frustration and fascination. Early on, my attempts felt more like fumbles—too dark, too bland, just not quite right. But with each shutter click, I pieced together the intricate puzzle of lighting, angles, and expressions. My mission, refined through lots of trial and error, is simple: to empower you not just to take photos but to tell stories, to capture confidence, and to open doors.

"The Headshot Handbook," is your pathway from the foundational steps of lens selection and lighting setups to the nuanced art of engaging with your subject and capturing a photo that speaks volumes. Whether you're a budding photographer or a seasoned lens person looking to hone your focus on headshots, this guide is crafted for you.

What sets this book apart is the technical skills it imparts and the holistic approach it advocates. Photography, especially of people, isn't just about precision in lighting or sharpness of an image; it's about connecting, understanding your subject, and respecting the story they wish to tell through their gaze. Alongside practical advice, you'll find discussions on the psychology of photography, ethical considerations, and real-world strategies to transform your passion into a thriving business.

Structured so that each chapter builds upon the last, we'll start with the nuts and bolts of camera settings and lighting, advance through the subtleties of directing and capturing the essence of your subjects, and turn your passion into a profitable venture. Expect to close the last page proficient in technicalities, savvy in business strategies, and enriched with a deeper understanding of your creative expression.

As you turn each page, consider this a learning journey and an invitation to a community of like-minded photography enthusiasts. Share your breakthroughs, stunning captures, and even the hiccups. Together, we grow more robust and more capable.

So, as we embark on this journey together, remember that each headshot you take is more than a photograph. It's a frame of confidence, a snapshot of ambition, a portrait of dreams. Let's begin this journey with an open mind and an eager heart, ready to explore headshot photography's mechanics and magic.

Let the adventure begin!

Chapter 1: Mastering the Basics of Headshot Photography

Have you ever met someone who swears by their decade-old camera, claiming it captures souls, not just smiles? A kernel of truth is buried there—great photography isn't just about owning the latest shiny gear. It's about knowing your tools like the back of your hand and using them to spin ordinary moments into visual poetry. In this chapter, we'll strip down the glitz of brand names and focus on what makes a headshot stand out. We're not just talking about picking a camera and snapping a pic; we're exploring how to choose equipment that works as hard as you do, ensuring every shutter's click counts.

Choosing Your Gear: Beyond the Brand Names

Let's start by getting honest about what you need to capture those eye-popping headshots. It's easy to fall into the trap of thinking you need the most expensive camera and lens to shoot like the pros. But here's a little secret: the best photographers could probably shoot stunning headshots with a potato if they had to. It's not just about the gear; it's about how you use it.

Understanding Needs Over Wants

First, let's differentiate between what you need and what the flashy advertisements make you think you need. Starting with the basics is crucial for beginners—a reliable camera and a versatile lens. You don't need a whole arsenal—just something solid to learn the ropes. As you grow more comfortable and your skills sharpen, you add specialized tools to your kit.

Conversely, professionals will need gear that can keep up with their advanced demands—fast autofocus for capturing crisp details, high resolution for print-quality photos, and robust build quality to withstand the rigors of daily use. Each piece of equipment is a long-term investment, enhancing your ability to tell stories through your portraits.

Lens Selection for Clarity and Bokeh

Now, let's talk lenses. Prime lenses are your best friends in the headshot game. Why? They're notorious for their ability to churn out images sharper than a samurai sword. Plus, they offer beautiful bokeh—that creamy, out-of-focus background that makes your subject pop like a 3D movie. A classic 85mm prime lens is a staple for headshot photographers due to its flattering compression and minimal distortion. It's like the lens was born to make people look good.

But pay attention to the humble 50mm lens. It's versatile,

typically more affordable, and fantastic for tighter spaces. Its natural perspective makes for comfortable, relatable shots where the subject is chatting with the viewer.

Camera Bodies With the Right Features

Moving on to camera bodies, remember that not all cameras are created equal, and the best one depends heavily on what you're shooting. For headshots, prioritize high resolution and excellent low-light performance. This combination will allow you to capture every pore and eyelash, which is crucial when your goal is to get up close and personal without losing quality or introducing noise.

Then there's autofocus. In the fast-paced world of headshot photography, where micro-expressions last but a millisecond, a camera with snappy autofocus is invaluable. It's like having a co-pilot who's got your back, ensuring you never miss that perfect, fleeting smirk.

Accessories That Make a Difference

Lastly, let's remember the unsung heroes: the accessories. A sturdy tripod can be your rock when aiming for precision in your shots. It eliminates camera shake and frees you up to focus on interacting with your subject rather than worrying about holding your camera steady.

Next up are the reflectors. These nifty tools bounce light back onto your subject, illuminating unwanted shadows and high-lighting those killer cheekbones. They're simple, effective, and can dramatically elevate the quality of natural-light headshots.

And let's give a quick shout-out to remote triggers. These gadgets allow you to take photos without touching your camera—perfect for keeping it still during those crucial shots or when you want to step away and direct your subject without running back to your camera after every adjustment.

Understanding and selecting the right gear set the stage for headshot magic. It's not about having the best of everything but the tools that work best for you and your vision of capturing stunning headshots that speak volumes.

Understanding Lighting: The Key to Transformative Headshots

Imagine you're at a cozy coffee shop at sunrise, the golden light spilling over your espresso, casting long, dramatic shadows. That, my friends, is the magic of lighting—it can turn the mundane into something spectacular. Now, imagine harnessing that kind of magic in your headshots. That's what we're aiming for. Let's break down the lighting basics, not just to illuminate but to sculpt and tell a story with each headshot.

Fundamentals of Lighting

Lighting in photography is like seasoning in cooking. Just as the right spices enhance a dish, lighting can transform a headshot. You'll deal with three main types of light: key light, fill light, and backlight. The key is your leading light, usually positioned slightly to one side of the camera. It lights up your subject's face. Think of it as the lead singer in a band—grabbing most of the attention.

Next up, fill the light. It's like the harmony to your lead singer, softening and eliminating unwanted shadows caused by the vital light without overpowering it. Usually, this light is less intense and placed opposite the key light. It's all about balance, ensuring the face has enough light to reveal details without washing out the contours.

Backlight, or rim light, is the unsung hero that can pop your subject off the background by creating a subtle glow or halo around their edges. It adds depth and dimension, making the headshot feel more three-dimensional. Placed behind the subject, this light outlines them with a light edge, which is particularly helpful if the background is dark.

Manipulating Natural Light

Natural light is like a box of chocolates—you never quite know what you'll get, making it exciting and unpredictable. The key is flexibility and adaptation. The best natural light for headshots can often be found during the golden hours, shortly after sunrise or before sunset, when the light is soft, diffused, and just plain flattering. Position your subject so the light falls on their face in a way that highlights their features without causing them to squint or create harsh shadows.

On overcast days, the clouds act like a giant softbox, scattering light evenly and creating a soft, shadow-less light. It's perfect for headshots as it minimizes wrinkles and imperfections.

Always be aware of your surroundings and how the sun's position affects the light. Sometimes, simply moving your subject a few feet can drastically change the quality of the light and, consequently, the photo.

Introduction to Artificial Lighting

Diving into artificial lighting might seem like stepping into a labyrinth, but it's easier than you think. A simple setup with one light and a reflector can yield stunning results. The idea is to use the artificial light as your key light, positioning it at about a 45-degree angle from your subject, mimicking the natural light of the golden hour. Use a softbox or an umbrella to diffuse the light, softening the shadows and making the light wrap around the subject's face more naturally.

As you grow more comfortable, you can add more lights, experimenting with fill and backlight to enhance the depth and drama of your headshots. Remember, the goal is not just to light your subject but to shape the light to fit the mood and purpose of the headshot.

Lighting Setups for Mood

Lighting can dramatically alter the mood of a headshot. Want to convey power and drama? Go for low-key lighting with stark contrasts and deep shadows. This setup often uses more robust, directional lighting to create a bold, intense look. On the flip side, with its bright and airy feel, high-key lighting uses lots of diffuse light to create a more approachable, friendly image.

Each lighting type tells a different story. It's like choosing the background music for a scene in a movie. The light's intensity, direction, and quality all contribute to the emotional response you want to evoke from the viewer. Whether you want your subject to appear strong, vulnerable, mysterious, or open, lighting is your path to achieving that emotional impact.

By understanding these lighting fundamentals and learning to manipulate both natural and artificial light, you're well on your way to creating headshots that do more than show a face —they show a personality, a mood, and a story. And isn't that the kind of magic we all want to create?

Composition and Framing: Making Every Shot Count

If you've ever caught yourself gazing at a photo where everything seems to click, chances are, you've witnessed the magic of stellar composition and framing. Like those headshots where the person's eyes pierce through the paper or screen, beckoning a visual dialogue? That's no happy accident. It's the result of meticulous crafting of the image, where every element works harmoniously to draw your focus exactly where it needs to be— on the subject. In this section, we're peeling back the layers of this visual symphony, exploring how the rule of thirds, angles, perspectives, and thoughtful framing combine to elevate a simple headshot into a compelling story.

The Rule of Thirds in Headshots

Let's chat about the rule of thirds because it's the bread and butter of photo composition. Imagine breaking an image down into a tic-tac-toe board. Two horizontal lines and two vertical lines intersect, creating nine equal squares. The rule of thirds posits that placing your subject along these lines or at their intersections creates more tension, energy, and interest in the composition than placing the subject smack dab in the center.

Now, apply this to headshots. Positioning the eyes along the top horizontal line ensures they are a focal point and imbues the photo with balance and direction. It feels natural to us as viewers because it mimics how we naturally see the world, not in halves but thirds. This technique is particularly potent in headshots because it pulls the viewer into a direct engagement with the subject's gaze, creating a connection that feels both intentional and inviting.

Using Angles and Perspectives

Have you ever tilted your head to get a new perspective on something? Well, the same concept can dramatically alter the impact of a headshot. Shooting from above for instance can make the subject seem smaller or more vulnerable, which could be perfect for a character actor looking to play a sympathetic role. Conversely, shooting from a lower angle makes the subject look more authoritative and dominant, ideal for corporate headshots or roles demanding a robust and assertive presence.

It's all about the story you want to tell. Changing your angle and perspective can bring a mundane shot to life, imbuing it with character and depth. It's like choosing the narrator for a novel; the story changes depending on who tells it and where they stand.

Framing for Impact

Imagine walking through a lush garden and spotting a stunning flower. How you frame it with the leaves around it can highlight its beauty or leave it lost among the foliage. Similarly, in headshots, how you frame your subject can significantly affect how the viewer perceives them. Environmental elements like archways, door frames, or even pulled-back curtains can add a natural depth to the shot and draw the viewer's eye directly to the subject.

Props play a big part here, too. For example, a musician might be framed by their instrument, adding context and depth to the headshot and telling a mini-narrative about the subject's passion and skills. This technique enhances the visual appeal and layers the headshot with additional meaning and character, making the subject more memorable.

Balancing the Shot

Balancing a headshot is akin to a chef balancing flavors in a dish. Just as too much salt can overpower a meal, too much clutter or imbalance in a headshot can detract from the subject. The goal is to compose the elements to complement rather than compete with the subject. This could mean adjusting the subject's position within the frame, changing your background, or even altering the lighting to ensure the subject is the undisputed star of the shot. It's about creating a visual equilibrium that feels both pleasing and intentional.

Consider everything within the frame—every line, shadow, and shape—as part of a whole. Each element should contribute to a cohesive story, with the subject as the protagonist. When everything is balanced, the viewer's eye can travel smoothly around the frame, always returning to the focal point—the subject's face or eyes—without effort or confusion.

By mastering the rule of thirds, experimenting with angles and perspectives, thoughtfully framing your subject, and balancing the visual elements within your shot, you equip yourself with the tools to turn every headshot into a work of art. These techniques are guidelines and pathways to deeper storytelling through your photography, allowing each headshot to capture an image and captivate an audience.

The Psychology Behind a Successful Headshot

Diving into the world of headshot photography isn't just about nailing focus or managing light; it's about capturing a fragment of the soul. Sounds deep, but it's true. The essence of a genuinely impactful headshot lies in its ability to reveal something profound about the subject, something that resonates with the viewer on an emotional level. Let's peel back the layers of how understanding your subject's personality and aspirations can dramatically steer the direction of your headshot session.

Capturing the Essence of the Subject

Think about a headshot as a story contained in a single frame. Every person stepping before your lens has a unique story filled with dreams, achievements, and aspirations. Your job? To translate that narrative into a visual format. Start by chatting with your subject before the shoot. What are they passionate about? What message do they want to convey through their headshot? Are they aiming for an approachable vibe or something more commanding? This isn't just idle chitchat; crucial reconnaissance will dictate everything from your lighting setup to your chosen angle and framing. For instance, a corporate executive might benefit from a robust, straight-on angle to denote authority, while an artist might prefer a softer, more abstract composition that hints at creativity. You create a visible and felt headshot by aligning your photographic approach with their narrative.

The Photographer-Subject Connection

Now, onto building rapport. This is where your interpersonal skills shine. Establishing a connection with your subject is paramount. It's about making them feel seen and comfortable, allowing them to drop guard and present their most authentic selves to the camera. Use humor, empathy, and active listening. Be present. It's incredible how genuinely connecting can transform a stiff, lifeless session into a dynamic and powerful one. When your subject trusts you, they relax. And a relaxed subject who can laugh at your bad jokes? That's someone ready to give you the natural expressions that make for a killer headshot.

The Impact of a Headshot

Consider the power of a well-executed headshot. It's not just a photograph; it's a key that can open doors to new opportunities. It could mean the difference between landing an audition or not for actors. For professionals, it represents their brand in a competitive marketplace. A headshot can convey confidence, approachability, professionalism, or charisma. It tells the viewer, within mere seconds, who the subject is and what they stand for. That's a lot of responsibility resting on your shoulders, right? Absolutely. But with the right approach, it's a challenge that transforms into an opportunity to significantly impact someone's career and self-perception.

Emotional Intelligence in Photography

Last but certainly not least, let's talk about emotional intelligence in photography. Reading the non-verbal cues of your subjects is like having a superpower. It tells you when to push for more intensity in their expression, back off, and give them a moment. It's about observing those slight frowns, the subtle shifts in posture, and adjusting your direction accordingly. Your subject is getting tired, and that energetic vibe you were going for is starting to wane. That's your cue to crack a joke, let them relax, or it's time to wrap up the session. Being attuned to these details not only ensures you meet their needs but also enhances the comfort and overall experience of the shoot, culminating in genuine expressions that are gold for any headshot.

In essence, understanding and connecting with your subject, recognizing the profound impact of your work, and harnessing your emotional intelligence are not just supplementary skills but central tenets of successful headshot photography. They transform a simple click of the shutter into a meaningful, career-enhancing, and sometimes life-changing moment. So, as you line up your next shot, remember, you're not just framing a face; you're framing a future. Keep this mindset, watch your photographs tell more profound stories, your sessions become more fulfilling, and your portfolio grows in size and substance.

Essential Camera Settings for Perfect Headshots

Dive into the world of camera settings, and you may be learning a new language. But fear not! Think of ISO, aperture, and shutter speed as the Holy Trinity of photography—they control everything from brightness to blur, transforming your photos from amateur snaps to professional portraits. Let's break down these settings to see how they can make or break your headshots.

ISO, Aperture, and Shutter Speed

First up, ISO—a setting that might sound more like a new tech startup than something that belongs in your camera. In layman's terms, ISO controls your camera sensor's sensitivity to light. Low ISO numbers (like 100 or 200) mean less sensitivity, which is excellent for those bright, sunny days when light is abundant. High ISO numbers (like 1600 or 3200) boost your sensor's sensitivity to light, which is a lifesaver in dim settings. But beware, the higher you go, the more you risk introducing noise (those pesky, grainy dots) into your images. It's like seasoning food; the right amount can enhance, but too much can spoil the dish.

Then we have the aperture, which you can think of as the pupil of your camera lens. Like your pupils expand or contract to let in more or less light, changing the aperture adjusts the amount of light hitting the camera sensor. Aperture sizes are measured in f-stops—lower numbers like f/1.4 mean a wider aperture, great for letting in a lot of light and achieving that dreamy, blurred background (bokeh) that makes your subject stand out. Higher numbers like f/16 narrow the aperture, keeping more of the scene in focus, which is less ideal for headshots where you want your subject to be the clear star of the show.

Shutter speed is the speedster of the group, controlling how long the camera shutter stays open to expose the sensor to light. Fast shutter speeds (1/500th of a second) are perfect for freezing motion, ensuring every hair and eyelash is pin-sharp. Slow shutter speeds (like 1/30th of a second), on the other hand, can lead to blurring from even the slightest movement. Sticking to faster shutter speeds is usually your best bet for headshots, where even a tiny twitch can turn a perfect shot into a blurry mess.

Using Aperture to Control Depth of Field

Let's zoom in on the aperture a bit more—specifically, how it helps control the depth of field. Depth of field is all about how much of your shot is in sharp focus. With a wider aperture (remember, that's a lower f-stop number), you get a shallower depth of field. This is fantastic for headshots because it blurs out the background, making your subject pop like they're 3D. It shifts all the attention right where you want it—on your subject. In comparison, a smaller aperture (a higher f-stop number) would keep more of the background in focus, which can be distracting in a headshot. It's like when you're at a party and want to listen to one person speaking; you don't need to hear everyone else's conversations!

Shutter Speed and Avoiding Blur

On to our friend, shutter speed. When capturing headshots, sharpness is non-negotiable. You want to see the sparkle in the eyes, the subtle textures of the skin—you want it all crystal clear. This clarity is where your choice of shutter speed plays a critical role. Too slow, and you risk blurring; too fast, and you might underexpose your image if the lighting isn't adequate. A good rule of thumb for headshots? Start with a shutter speed of at least 1/200th of a second. This speed tends to be fast enough to freeze any minor movements from your subject. It's like snapping a photo of a dancer mid-pose—you capture the grace without the motion.

ISO and Noise Considerations

Finally, let's get back to ISO. The goal is to keep it as low as possible to minimize noise, which can detract from your headshot's overall quality and professionalism. However, lighting conditions only sometimes cooperate. In cases where you're losing light but need to avoid blur, incrementally increasing your ISO is practical. It's about finding that spot where you have enough light to keep your shutter speed fast and your aperture set for a shallow depth of field without cranking up the ISO so high that the image becomes too noisy. Sometimes, it's a bit of a balancing act—a photography dance, if you will.

Understanding and manipulating these settings to your advantage will equip you with the tools to take headshots that are not only technically sound but also strikingly impactful. It's about harmonizing ISO, aperture, and shutter speed to create a visual symphony that draws viewers in and holds their gaze, one stunning headshot at a time.

Navigating Natural vs. Studio Light: A Comprehensive Guide

Ah, the eternal dance between natural and studio lighting—each has its charm and challenges, like choosing between a classic vinyl record and a crisp digital download. Understanding how to use both effectively is akin to a chef mastering cooking over an open flame and an induction stove. Each method brings out different flavors and nuances in the dish.

Advantages and Challenges of Natural Light

With its golden hues and soft shadows, natural light can bring warmth and authenticity to headshots that are hard to replicate artificially. How natural light wraps around the subject can make your photos feel alive, almost as if they could step out of the frame. It's perfect for creating a welcoming, approachable vibe. However, it's not without its pitfalls. The main challenge? Its unpredictability. You're at the mercy of the weather, time of day, and cloud cover, which can change your lighting setup in the blink of an eye.

To harness the beauty of natural light while mitigating its

variability, timing is everything. Overcast days are fantastic for shooting as the clouds act like a giant diffuser, creating a soft, even light that minimizes harsh shadows. If you're aiming for more dramatic lighting, the golden hours—shortly after sunrise or before sunset—are ideal. The light is warmer and more directional, giving you those long, dramatic shadows that can add depth and intrigue to your headshots. The key is flexibility; sometimes, you must move fast, chase the light, or find shade to achieve the best illumination for your subject.

Transitioning to Studio Lights

Moving into studio lighting can feel like learning to drive a manual car after years of automatic—it gives you more control, but there's a bit of a learning curve. Studio lights are your best friends when consistency and control are top priorities. Whether it's a sunny day or a stormy evening, studio lights give you the same result every time. But where do you start?

Setting up your first studio light setup doesn't have to be daunting. Begin with a simple one-light setup. Place your key light at a 45-degree angle to your subject, slightly above their eye level, to mimic natural light. This setup minimizes weird shadows and highlights the facial features beautifully. As you grow more comfortable, you can add a fill light to soften shadows and a backlight to help separate the subject from the background, adding depth to your headshots. Remember, the goal of studio lighting isn't to flood your subjects with light but to sculpt their features in a natural and flattering way.

Combining Natural and Artificial Light

Now, for a bit of magic—combining natural and artificial light. This technique can help you achieve the best of both worlds—the authenticity and warmth of natural light with the control and consistency of studio lighting. The trick is to balance these light sources to complement each other rather than compete. Start with setting up your artificial light to mimic the natural light in your space. If you have a solid directional light from a window, match your studio light to follow the same direction and quality of light. Use diffusers or bounce cards to soften the artificial light to ensure it blends seamlessly with the natural light, avoiding any harsh shadows or apparent signs of artificial lighting.

Solving Common Lighting Problems

Even with the best setups, lighting problems can arise. Harsh shadows and flat lighting are common culprits that can detract from an otherwise perfect headshot. Employ a reflector for harsh shadows, particularly those under the chin or around the nose. Position it opposite your primary light source to bounce light back onto the shadowed areas, softly filling them in without erasing natural contours. It's like using a gentle eraser to soften pencil lines in a sketch, maintaining integrity while enhancing the overall effect.

Flat lighting, whose features appear two-dimensional and lack depth, often occurs when the light source is too direct or diffused. To combat this, adjust the angle of your light. Moving it to the side or having it come from above can reintroduce those subtle shadows that give the face form and character. It's about finding that sweet spot where the light flatters but doesn't overpower, highlighting the subject's best features while preserving the depth that makes a headshot dynamic and engaging.

By mastering these techniques, you can take control of your lighting environment, whether basking in the sun's glow or crafting light in the studio. Each setting offers unique opportunities to shape light creatively around your subject, enhancing not just their features but the very mood and atmosphere of your headshots. Remember, good lighting is not just about visibility—it's about vision. It's about using light to tell a story, evoke an emotion, and capture a moment that feels real and extraordinary.

Directing 101: Getting the Best Out of Your Subject

When diving into the world of headshot photography, think of yourself not just as a photographer but as a director. You're or-chestrating a scene, setting the stage for your subjects to shine. It's your job to pull out the most engaging, authentic version of them, which requires a cocktail of comfort, communication, and a keen eye for body language. Let's unpack some secrets to mastering this delicate dance, ensuring every subject feels like a star ready for their close-up.

Establishing Comfort and Confidence

Creating a comfortable atmosphere starts the moment your subject walks through the door. Kick-off with a warm greeting and a genuine compliment. It's about making them feel seen, not just as subjects, but as people. Keep the vibe light; a little humor goes a long way. Then, dive into a casual chat before the shoot. Discuss their day, interests, or the music playing in the background. This isn't just small talk—it's your tool to gauge their mood and comfort level, making mental notes on how to approach their session.

As you start shooting, keep the conversation flowing. A silent studio can make the click of each shutter feel like a thunderclap. Talk about what poses feel most natural to them, or ask them to think about a pleasant memory, which can bring a natural smile and spark in their eyes. Show them a few shots on the camera to boost their confidence and involve them in the process. It's a collaboration, after all. Their feedback can guide you to adjust and capture their best angles and expressions.

Verbal and Non-Verbal Direction

Clear, concise directions are your best friend. Use straight-forward language to guide their poses. Phrases like "tilt your head slightly" or "lower your chin just a bit" are easy to follow and execute. But it's not just about what you say; it's how you say it. Your tone should be encouraging, and your instructions should be sprinkled with affirmations like "That looks great!" or "You're doing awesome."

Non-verbal cues are equally potent. Sometimes, demonstrating a pose yourself can clear up any confusion and lighten the mood. Other times, a simple gesture—pointing to where they should look or giving a thumbs up—can communicate your thoughts more clearly than words. Be mindful of your body language, too. Maintain an open, relaxed posture to mirror the ease you want them to feel.

The Role of Body Language

Understanding and utilizing your subject's body language can transform a good shot into a great one. Start by observing their natural stance. Are they holding tension in their shoulders? Do they habitually tilt their head in a specific direction? These cues can guide your direction, helping you adjust your posture naturally yet flatteringly.

Encourage them to breathe deeply if they seem tense, which can relax their facial muscles and shoulders. Use their hands to create natural, engaging poses. Have them hook a thumb in their jeans or play with their hair. These small actions help reduce stiffness and add a layer of personality and movement to the shots.

Practical Posing Tips

Now, let's talk about the cheat sheet of poses. Having a set of go-to poses can make directing smoother, especially when working with non-models. Start with a straight-on shot, a three-quarter turn, and a profile. From there, adjust based on the subject's body type and comfort. For instance, if someone is self-conscious about their height, shooting from a slightly elevated angle can make them appear taller, boosting their confidence.

Encourage subjects to shift their weight from one foot to another. This simple motion can create a more dynamic pose, giving the final shot an impression of movement and liveliness. For those more reserved, closed poses—like arms crossed or hands gently folded in their lap—can make them feel more secure and composed.

Remember, the best pose is the one that feels right for the subject. It's about enhancing their natural stature and personality, not forcing them into awkward, unnatural positions. By building a rapport, communicating clearly, and using body language effectively, you make your subjects comfortable and bring out their best, capturing headshots that are both striking and true to who they are. As you guide each subject through their poses, keep an eye on the nuances of their expressions and adjust your approach to capture their unique essence. Every click of the shutter allows you to explore new angles, experiment with different expressions, and refine your technique. This proactive, attentive direction enhances the quality of your headshots and ensures a rewarding experience for you and your subjects.

The Art of Background Selection: Enhancing Your Subject

When it comes to headshot photography, think of the background as the unsung hero of your photo. It's the silent supporter, setting the stage for your subject, enhancing their features, and either elevating the story you're trying to tell or, if chosen poorly, completely derailing it. The right background can add depth, context, and intrigue to your headshots, turning what could be a standard shot into something truly memorable. Let's dive into how you can select and utilize backgrounds that complement rather than compete with your subject.

Choosing the fitting backdrop is akin to picking the right outfit for an interview—it should enhance your appearance, not distract from it. Start by considering what you want the headshot to convey. Is it professionalism for a corporate lawyer, creativity for a graphic designer, or approachability for a pediatrician? Each of these will benefit from different backdrops. For instance, a simple, uncluttered background works wonders for professional headshots as it directs all attention to the subject. On the other hand, an artist might benefit from a more textured, colorful background that hints at their creative nature.

The environment around you is a treasure trove of potential backgrounds. An old brick wall can provide a textured, exciting backdrop with a rustic feel to the shot, perfect for someone in a creative or artisan field. For a more corporate or professional look, opt for cleaner lines and muted colors, like the side of a modern building or a plain-colored wall. The key here is to always keep the focus on the subject. The background should be like a good bass line in a song—felt but not overtaking the lead vocals.

Now, let's talk about bokeh. Bokeh comes from a Japanese word meaning blur. In photography, it refers to the beautiful out-of-focus light points that occur when shooting with a shallow depth of field. This technique is perfect for headshots because it isolates your subject from the background, making them the focal point. Achieving pleasing bokeh involves using a fast lens—at least f/2.8, but the faster, the better, like f/1.4. Open up that aperture, and position your subject at a reasonable distance from the background while keeping them close to the camera. This setup maximizes the blur effect on the background, beautifully encapsulating your subject in a soft, gentle wash of light and color that makes them pop.

Incorporating environmental elements creatively can transform a plain background into a storytelling element. For instance, positioning a musician with their instrument in front of a graffiti-covered wall can convey a sense of edginess and artistry, resonating with their brand. For outdoor settings, elements like trees can frame the subject naturally, or benches can add a casual, relaxed feel. Every environment component should serve a purpose by adding context, enhancing the mood, or focusing more on the subject's personality.

Consistency is critical when aligning the background with the subject matter. The background should complement the subject's brand and the purpose of the headshot. If you're shooting a headshot for a corporate executive, a chaotic, brightly colored background might send the wrong message. Instead, opt for something understated and professional. Conversely, for a yoga instructor, a background that conveys tranquility and connection with nature, like a calm lake or a serene park, can enhance the peaceful vibe they want to communicate.

Remember, the goal of a great headshot is to tell a part of the subject's story before they even speak. Every choice, from the background to the lighting, plays a crucial role in crafting this narrative. By selecting a background that enhances rather than distracts, using techniques like bokeh to focus on the subject, creatively incorporating environmental elements, and aligning the background with the subject's brand, you transform a simple photograph into a powerful tool that captures and conveys the individual's unique essence. This thoughtful approach ensures that each headshot you take looks professional and resonates emotionally and contextually with its intended audience, making every shot a compelling piece of visual storytelling.

Building Confidence Behind the Camera: Tips and Tricks

There's something magical about the moment you pick up a camera and realize it's not just a piece of technology but a gateway to capturing the essence of the world around you. But let's be honest—initially, that camera can feel more like a Rubik's cube, especially when trying to nail perfect headshots. Confidence behind the lens doesn't just sprout overnight; it's cultivated through a blend of knowledge, preparation, deliberate practice, and open-hearted learning from feedback. So, let's break down these elements that build the confidence that transforms good photographers into great ones.

Knowledge Breeds Confidence

First up, let's talk about getting to know your gear. Understanding the ins and outs of your camera is like learning every secret pathway in your favorite video game; it gives you an edge, and using your equipment becomes second nature. Spend time with your camera manual—yes, it might not be a page-turner, but it's packed with nuggets of gold that can elevate your shooting skills. Know what each button does, how to change your settings quickly, and what to do when things don't look right. Familiarize yourself with terms like ISO, shutter speed, and aperture, and learn how they affect your images. This isn't just technical jargon; it's the language of photography, and understanding it means you can more effectively bring your creative vision to life.

Preparation is Key

Let's chat about preparation because winging might work for a spontaneous road trip but less for professional photography. Before a shoot, check all your gear. Charge your batteries, clean your lenses, and make sure you have all the necessary equipment packed. Think about your shooting location and the light conditions you expect. Are you planning your shoot around natural light? Remember, the sun waits for no one, so timing is crucial. Make a shot list or a mood board to help clarify the look and feel you aim for. This helps keep you organized and serves as a visual reminder of your shoot goals.

Pre-shoot communication with your subject is equally important. Discuss what they should wear, how they should prepare, and what they hope to achieve with the shoot. This prep talk can ease the subject's nerves and give you insights into how best to capture their personality and essence. It's like doing homework before a big test—it can significantly boost your confidence because you've laid down a solid foundation to build upon.

Practicing with Purpose

Let's pivot to the heart of skill-building: practice. But not just any practice—purposeful practice. This means setting specific goals for each session, such as working on capturing sharper images, experimenting with different lighting setups, or mastering directing your subjects. It's about quality, not just quantity. Shoot regularly, but also reflectively. Try different genres of photography to develop adaptability and bring fresh perspectives to your headshots. Shoot in various lighting conditions to challenge yourself and deepen your understanding of how light works. Remember, every pro was once an amateur who kept learning and pushing their craft's boundaries.

Feedback and Growth

Lastly, let's talk about the goldmine, which is constructive feedback. It can come from mentors, peers, or even clients. Encourage honest critiques and be open to hearing what could be improved. Yes, praise is easier on the ears, but constructive criticism is where actual growth happens. Join photography groups, participate in workshops, and share your work online to engage with a community that supports and challenges you. Reflect on the feedback, and use it as a stepping stone to refine your techniques and approach.

Moreover, self-evaluation is a powerful tool. After each shoot, take the time to review your images critically. Ask yourself what worked, what didn't, and why. This kind of self-reflection can accelerate your growth exponentially, turning experiences, good and bad, into valuable lessons.

Building confidence behind the camera is a journey of continuous learning and adaptation. It's about embracing the process, celebrating the small victories, and constantly pushing forward, knowing that each step takes you closer to the masterful execution of your art. So, grab your camera, dive into the learning, and shoot with the heart of a student and the mind of a seasoned pro. As you do, watch your confidence and portfolio grow richer with each shutter click.

Common Mistakes and How to Avoid Them

Let's face it—we've all had those "Oops!" moments in photography where something so essential slips through the cracks, leaving us with a facepalm-worthy result. From overcooked editing to missing a sneaky photobomber in the background, these blunders can be learning opportunities—or repeated frustrations. Here, I'll guide you through some common missteps in headshot photography and how to sidestep them gracefully, ensuring your photos look top-notch every single time.

Overprocessing in Post-Editing

Ah, the digital darkroom, where raw photos go to turn into magazine-worthy masterpieces—or where they're overcooked into oblivion. It's tempting to slide those sliders to the max. Brightness up, contrast full blast, skin smoothed to porcelain doll levels. But here's the rub: over-editing can strip away your headshots' natural character and depth, leaving you with something that looks more like a 3D render than a human being. The trick is to enhance, not overshadow. Use editing tools to correct and subtly improve, not to transform completely. Think of it as makeup—enough to highlight the best features, not so much that it looks like a mask. Keep skin texture natural, retain the catchlights in the eyes, and avoid going overboard with color saturation. Sometimes, less is indeed more.

Ignoring the Subject's Input

Remember, a headshot session is a collaboration, not a dictatorship. Ignoring your subject's input can lead to a photo they're happier with and a missed opportunity to capture their true essence. It's vital to check in with your subject throughout the shoot. Ask if they have any poses they feel comfortable with or if there are any aspects of their appearance they'd like to highlight or downplay. This dialogue doesn't just help capture photos that resonate more with the subject, but it also makes them feel valued and understood, which in turn helps them relax and show their best self in front of the camera. Their ideas might surprise you and bring a fresh perspective to your work!

Neglecting the Details

Ah, the devil's in the details, as they say. A stray hair across the face, a wrinkled shirt, and an awkwardly placed accessory can all distract from an otherwise stellar headshot. Keep an eagle eye on these little details throughout the shoot. It's helpful to take a few moments to scan the subject from head to toe before pressing the shutter. Look for anything amiss—adjust ties, smooth down flyaway hairs, and straighten out collars. Consider keeping a small grooming kit on hand for quick fixes. Paying attention to these small elements can vastly improve the quality of your headshots and save you a headache in post-processing trying to fix things that could have been quickly addressed during the shoot.

Failing to Check the Background

It is never taken what you thought was a perfect headshot, only to find later that there's a tree seemingly sprouting from the subject's head. Backgrounds can make or break your headshots. Always take a moment to review what's behind your subject. Look for distractions like bright colors, high-contrast patterns, or objects that could appear awkwardly positioned about the subject. A simple shift in your shooting angle or asking the subject to move a few steps can often solve these issues. Remember, the background should never compete with the subject; it should complement and help them stand out.

Navigating these common pitfalls can significantly enhance the quality and impact of your headshots. By respecting the subject's input, maintaining attention to detail, cautiously editing, and vigilantly selecting your backgrounds, you ensure that your headshots look professional, polished, and genuinely representative of the subject's personality. These practices refine your technical skills and enrich your interpersonal interactions, making your photography sessions more enjoyable and productive for everyone involved.

Chapter 2: Advanced Lighting Techniques for Indoor and Outdoor Headshots

Lighting, my dear reader, is the secret sauce of photography. Get it right, and you have a masterpiece that can make the Mona Lisa smile wider. Get it wrong, and you might end up with a collection of glorified passport photos. So, let's roll up our sleeves and dive into the enchanting world of indoor lighting, where we control the Sun with the flick of a switch and create depth and emotion with the placement of a bulb. This chapter is your backstage pass to mastering the light, manipulating shadows, and making every headshot a window to the soul.

Crafting the Perfect Indoor Lighting Setup

Layering Light Sources for Balance

Imagine you're a conductor at an orchestra; each musician (or light source, in our case) has a role to play in creating harmony.

In photography, this harmony is achieved by skillfully balancing key light, fill light, and backlight. Start with your key light—this is your lead violinist, setting the tone. Position it at a 45-degree angle from your subject, slightly above their eye level, to mimic how natural light falls on a face, creating a flattering, dimensional look.

Next, bring in the fill light—think of it as the cellos supporting the melody. Place it on the key light's opposite side, dialing down to about half the intensity. Its job isn't to eliminate shadows (which add depth and interest) but to soften them, preventing harsh contrasts that can age your subject or distort their features.

Finally, the backlight, our flutes, if you will, adds a subtle brilliance. Positioned behind the subject, it lifts them from the backdrop, adding a halo effect that is nothing short of divine. This separation is crucial in giving your subject their stage in the frame.

Choosing the Right Modifiers

Modifiers are like the spices in your kitchen; they can dramatically change the flavor of your light. Softboxes and umbrellas are two of the most beloved tools in a photographer's kit, each affecting the light's quality differently. Softboxes are like a fine sieve, softening and directing the light precisely where you want it, which is perfect for creating soft, flattering light that wraps gently around your subject.

On the other hand, Umbrellas are the big, boisterous siblings of softboxes. They spread light far and wide, creating a broad, diffused light source that's great for a softer, more ambient feel, like a cozy light blanket. However, they're a bit harder to control than softboxes, so they might spill light where you don't want it.

Controlling Light Spill

Speaking of unwanted light spills, they're like that guest who shows up uninvited to a party—they need to be tactfully managed. Use flags or barn doors on your lights to keep the light focused precisely where you intend it. Think of it as putting blinders on a horse, keeping it on your chosen path. This control is crucial in maintaining the mood of your image and keeping the viewer's focus on the subject, not distracted by a brightly lit vase in the background.

Lighting Ratios for Mood

The ratio of key light to fill light can dramatically alter the mood of your headshots. A 1:1 ratio creates a flat, evenly lit face with equal key and fill. It's safe, but let's be honest, it's also a bit boring. Now, a 2:1 ratio—twice as much key light as fill light—now we're talking drama. It adds depth and contour to the face, perfect for an editorial look or someone who wants their headshot to pop with a bit of shadow play.

Pushing it to a 3:1 ratio intensifies this effect, deepening shadows and highlighting features, ideal for artistic or high-fashion shots. It's about balancing light like you balance flavors in a dish—too much salt, inedible, too little, and bland. Your job is to find the sweet spot that makes your subject look their best and conveys the right emotional tone for their headshot.

By understanding and manipulating these elements, you transform your studio into a playground of light. With each adjustment, you're not just illuminating a face; you're sculpting an image that can captivate, convince, and command attention. So, wield your lights like the powerful tools they are, and watch as each headshot you craft becomes a testament to your skill and vision.

Mastering Outdoor Lighting: Working with the Sun

Ah, the great outdoors—where the Sun is your studio lighting, and the world is your backdrop. But as any seasoned photographer will tell you, working with the sun isn't just about stepping outside and hoping for the best. It's about understanding its moods throughout the day and using them to your advantage. Let's break down how to harness this mighty star to cast your subjects in the best light.

Harnessing Golden Hour

Golden hour, that magical time just after sunrise or before sunset, is like nature's Instagram filter. It bathes everything in a warm, soft light that can make anyone look like they belong on the cover of a magazine. The sun's low angle during these times creates a flattering, diffused light that enhances skin tones and fills the eyes with a lively sparkle without harsh shadows. But here's the catch—it's fleeting, typically lasting only about an hour. To make the most of this precious time, plan. Scout your location in advance and know exactly where you want to shoot. Have your subject ready so you can go as soon as the light hits that sweet spot. Position your subject so the light falls gently across their face, either from the side or backlighting them for a sublime glow. Remember, timing is everything. Being even a few minutes late can mean missing out on the magic.

Managing Harsh Midday Light

Then there's the midday sun, a notorious time for photographers due to the strong overhead light that can cause unflattering shadows under the eyes and nose. But don't let the sun dictate your schedule. With a few tricks, you can tame this harsh light. Seeking shade is your first line of defense. Look for large trees, buildings, or other structures that provide a shadow large enough for your shoot. This natural diffuser helps soften the light. However, the shade can sometimes be too dark, which is where a reflector comes into play. Position a reflector to bounce some light back onto your subject, brightening up those shadows gently without reintroducing harshness. This setup can turn the dreaded high noon into a surprisingly good time for portraits.

Using the Sun as Backlight

Backlighting—where the sun is directly behind your subject— can turn an ordinary headshot into a heavenly shot. It creates a luminous outline around your subject, giving them an almost angelic halo that can be incredibly eye-catching. To achieve this, position your subject between the sun and yourself. You'll need to adjust your exposure settings to ensure your subject isn't just a silhouette unless that's the artistic look you're going for. Meter for the subject's face, and consider using a fill light or reflector to illuminate their features. This technique not only separates your subject from the background but also gives the image a lovely, ethereal quality that can't be replicated in a studio.

Overcast Conditions as a Natural Diffuser

Now, don't be dismayed by an overcast day; embrace it! Cloudy skies are nature's softbox—diffusing the sunlight and eliminating harsh shadows, making it an ideal condition for headshot photography. The even lighting flatters the skin and allows you to shoot at almost any time of the day without the drawbacks of solid shadows. However, the lower overall light levels might require adjusting your camera settings. Increase your ISO or open up your aperture to allow more light in. The beauty of overcast lighting is its consistency, giving you more time and flexibility to focus on composing your shot without racing against the changing sun.

Mastering outdoor lighting is about playing with the Sun's vast range of effects—from the golden warmth of its first and last light to the dramatic possibilities of its midday presence and the softness of an overcast day. Each brings challenges and opportunities, and as you grow more adept at navigating these conditions, you'll find that the sun can be one of the most versatile tools in your photographic toolkit, capable of transforming the mundane into the magnificent. With these strategies in your back pocket, you're well-equipped to capture headshots that are not only technically proficient but also stunningly beautiful.

High-Key and Low-Key Lighting Explained

Let's talk lighting moods, shall we? Imagine you're setting the scene for a movie. Each scene has a vibe, a tone that tells the audience how to feel. High-key and low-key lighting are your cinematic tools in photography, setting the emotional stage for your headshots. High-key lighting washes your scene with brightness, optimism, and an airy feel, while low-key does the opposite, dialing up the drama with shadows and contrast that could make even the cheeriest clown seem a bit mysterious. Understanding these styles and when to use them can turn your headshots from mere pictures into stories told in light.

Defining High-Key and Low-Key

High-key lighting is like the vibe of a sunny day at the beach— bright, clear, and devoid of drama. It's characterized by its ability to reduce shadows, featuring a light background and a very gentle contrast. It's fantastic for conveying positivity and an approachable persona. Think of a headshot for a therapist or a customer service manager, where trust and friendliness are critical.

On the other hand, low-key lighting is the coffee to high-key's cream. It's all about shadows and moodiness, often with a dark background and stark contrasts. This style is perfect for creating an air of mystery or sophistication—ideal for artistic types or roles that thrive on intensity and depth, like a stage actor or a jazz musician.

Setting Up for High-Key Lighting

Creating a high-key setup isn't just about blasting your subject with light; it's about control and balance. Start with a solid backdrop that's light in color, like white or pale gray. You'll want to use multiple light sources to light the backdrop evenly, eliminating shadows or gradients. This could mean using two lights on either side of the backdrop, angled to spread the light evenly.

For your subject, use a large softbox or umbrella to diffuse the light beautifully across their features, softening any shadows and bringing a gentle brightness to their face. Position this leading light slightly above and in front of your subject to ensure their features are well illuminated. You might also add a fill light opposite the leading light to gently lift any lingering shadows, keeping the fill light at about half the intensity of the main light. The goal is to keep the lighting soft and even, without harsh shadows that could introduce drama where you want serenity.

Achieving Low-Key Lighting

Ah, low-key lighting—it's all about the drama. For this setup, start with a dark backdrop to help absorb light rather than reflect it. You're aiming for a moody atmosphere, so embrace the darkness. Use a single light source to create stark contrasts. A snoot or grid can help you focus the light precisely where you want it, like sculpting with shadows. Position this light to the side or above and angled down at your subject to accentuate the texture and contours of their face, creating a play of light and shadow that's both dramatic and artistic.

Fill light? Keep it minimal or none at all. Remember, shadows are your friends here, adding depth and character to the headshot. You want those shadows to define the facial features and enhance the mood, not wash them out. This setup is perfect for someone with a strong, sculpted face, as it highlights bone structure and adds a layer of intrigue.

Applying These Styles to Headshots

Choosing between high-key and low-key lighting should be a deliberate decision based on what you want the headshot to communicate. High-key lighting is your go-to for headshots meant to suggest openness, sincerity, and safety—great for professionals who need to appear approachable and trustworthy. On the flip side, low-key lighting suits artistic fields or roles where mystery, creativity, or strength are celebrated. It's about matching the lighting style to your subject's personality and professional needs, using your understanding of light to enhance your story.

So, whether you're bathing your subject in light or sculpting them from the shadows, remember that your choice of lighting sets the tone for the headshot. It's not just about how they look but how they feel to the viewer. With high-key and low-key lighting, you can direct that emotional response, crafting headshots that do more than show; they tell.

Using Reflectors and Diffusers Like a Pro

Reflectors and diffusers are like the unsung heroes of the photography world, turning harsh lighting into your best friend and saving your shots on even the trickiest days. Let's kick off with reflectors. These nifty tools come in various colors and sizes, each with its unique effect on your subject. Silver reflectors are fantastic for adding a crisp, clean light to a scene, especially useful on cloudy days to mimic a bit of that bright sunlight. Gold reflectors, however, are like giving your subject a warm hug of light, perfect for sunset portraits or adding a golden-hour glow even when the Sun has other plans. White reflectors are more subtle, gently lifting shadows without changing the color temperature of the light. And for those times when you want to soften harsh shadows without adding much light, the translucent reflector, or diffuser, is your go-to tool, softening and spreading the light more evenly across the subject.

Now, positioning these reflectors is an art form in itself. It's not just about propping them up and hoping for the best; it's about sculpting the light to complement your subject. For fill light, place a silver or white reflector opposite your primary light source to bounce some of that light back onto the shadow side of your subject's face. This placement reduces contrast and illuminates details that might otherwise be lost in shadow. If you're looking to add a sparkle to their eyes—a catchlight— position a small reflector just below and in front of your subject. This placement catches the leading light and reflects it back into their eyes, making them come alive in the photograph.

Diffusers, those beautiful tools of subtlety, are your best friends on a bright, sunny day. Place a large diffuser between the sun and your subject to soften the harsh light, reducing squinting and harsh shadows that can mar an otherwise beautiful headshot. It's like placing a soft, translucent curtain between the sun and your subject, softening the intensity and spreading the light more uniformly. You can also use diffusers in the studio when your artificial lights are too harsh or direct. By softening the light, you create a more flattering, gentle illumination that can be much more forgiving on the skin.

For those of you on a budget, or if you're starting out and building your kit piece by piece, there are some ingenious DIY solutions to create effective reflectors and diffusers without breaking the bank. A simple piece of white cardboard can become a reflector with just a bit of aluminum foil taped to one side. This DIY silver reflector is great for adding a bit of fill light or creating catchlights. For a DIY diffuser, grab a white shower curtain or a piece of white fabric and stretch it tightly over a frame made from PVC pipes or even an old picture frame. Place it between your light source and your subject to soften harsh light. These homemade solutions are cost-effective and customizable to fit various shooting scenarios, proving that sometimes, a little creativity goes a long way in photography.

By mastering the use of reflectors and diffusers, you equip yourself with the ability to control and manipulate light in almost any environment, enhancing your ability to capture stunning headshots that look professionally lit, regardless of your surroundings. Whether using high-end gear or DIY solutions, the principles remain the same: soften harsh lights, fill in unwanted shadows, and use reflected light to add depth and dimension to your photographs. These tools are fundamental in helping you achieve that perfect balance of light and shadow, making each headshot a true work of art.

Creative Use of Shadows for Dramatic Effects

Shaping Light to Shape the Face

Let's talk about sculpting, but instead of clay or marble, your medium is light and shadow. The way you manipulate these elements can dramatically change the appearance and mood of your headshots. To create depth and bring out the best features in your subjects, consider the placement and quality of your shadows. It's not just about lighting up a face; it's about using shadows to enhance and define facial features. For instance, by positioning a light slightly to the side and above your subject, you create what we call 'Rembrandt lighting'— characterized by that iconic triangle of light on the cheek opposite the light source. This method not only adds volume and a classic feel but also accentuates cheekbones and jawlines, giving your subject a more defined, sculptural look in the photo.

The trick here is to balance the intensity and softness of your shadows. Too harsh, and your subject might end up looking older and more rugged than they might like (unless that's the mood you're going for). Too soft, and you might lose those defining lines that give the face character and depth. Play around with the distance and angle of your light sources to see how it changes the play of shadows across the face. A subtle shift can mean the difference between a flat portrait and one that pops with life and texture.

Creating Patterns with Light

Now, let's add some flair with patterns. By using gobos (go-betweens)—objects placed in front of your light source—you can cast intriguing shadows and patterns across your subject or background. This technique can add an artistic touch to your headshots, making them stand out in a sea of standard portraits. Imagine casting the delicate shadows of leaves across an actor's face, suggesting a role in a nature-themed play, or using geometric shapes to add a modern, edgy look to a musician's promo shots.

Creating these patterns isn't just about placing a random object in front of a light; it's about choosing shapes that complement the subject's personality or the story you want to tell. The size and distance of the gobo from the light source will affect the sharpness and scale of the patterns, so experiment with different setups. Remember, the goal is to enhance, not overpower. The patterns should add a layer of interest and meaning to the shot, not distract from the subject themselves.

Contrast as a Storytelling Tool

Contrast is your narrative brushstroke in the art of headshot photography. High contrast setups, where the difference between the lightest and darkest areas of the frame is pronounced, naturally draw the viewer's eye to lines and features, adding a dramatic, almost cinematic quality to your images. This technique works wonderfully for character portraits or headshots that aim to convey a strong, bold personality.

Think of a writer's promotional headshot, where the play of light and shadow across their face might mirror the thematic contrasts in their latest thriller novel. Or consider a dancer, where the dramatic lighting echoes their dramatic movements. In each case, the use of comparison does more than light a face; it tells a story, adding layers of depth and interest that speak of the subject's character and craft.

Avoiding Unwanted Shadows

While shadows can be your artistic allies, unwanted shadows can be just as much your foes. Unintended shadows under the eyes or chin can age your subject or give them a tired look, which is usually different from the goal. To mitigate this, always watch how light wraps around the face. Use reflectors or additional, softer light sources to fill these areas gently. Positioning your key light plays a crucial role here; even a slight adjustment can often shift a shadow from distracting to flattering.

Moreover, be mindful of the background. Shadows cast on

the background can create an unintended mood or look messy. This is where controlling your light spill becomes crucial. Use flags or adjust the angle of your light to keep the background as clean or as intentionally styled as you desire. Remember that every shadow casts a story in portrait photography, and controlling these visual elements should always serve the narrative you and your subject aim to tell.

Mastering these techniques enhances the technical prowess of your headshots and imbues them with a depth and drama that transcends the ordinary. By deliberately sculpting with light and shadow, creating engaging patterns, and utilizing contrast to tell stories, you transform your portraits into narratives captured in time, each shadow a brushstroke of your artistic vision.

Flash Photography for Compelling Headshots

Flash photography often gets a bad rap for making subjects look like deer caught in headlights. However, using a flash can transform your headshots from flat to fabulous when done right. Let's demystify the flash, starting with the basics and moving on to creative techniques to make your headshots pop.

Flash Basics for Beginners

For those just dipping their toes into the vast ocean of flash photography, let's start with understanding the two main types of flash: on-camera and off-camera. On-camera flash, as the name suggests, sits snugly on your camera. It's convenient and portable, but it can sometimes give you that dreaded passport photo look due to its direct, harsh light. This is where off- camera flash steps in to save the day. By moving the flash off to the side, you can control the direction and quality of the light much more effectively, allowing you to sculpt the light around your subject for a more flattering look.

Managing a flash isn't just about turning it on and firing away. You need to balance its power to suit the ambient light. This is key because you want to achieve a natural look that is not overly flashy. Start by setting your flash to lower power and take a test shot. Check if the subject is well-lit without overpowering the natural light. It's a bit like adding salt to a dish; you can always add more if needed, but too much initially can ruin the m eal.

Balancing Flash with Ambient Light

Balancing flash with ambient light is an art form that ensures your subject blends seamlessly into their surroundings. The goal is to use the flash to enhance the natural light, not compete with it subtly. To master this, you'll first need to meter the ambient light. Set your camera to manual mode and choose a combination of ISO, aperture, and shutter speed that gives you a well-exposed background. Then, introduce your flash, adjusting its power to fill in the shadows on your subject gently. This technique maintains the mood set by the ambient light while illuminating your subject just right, making the flash almost imperceptible.

Creative Flash Techniques

Once you're comfortable with the basics, it's time to play with some advanced flash techniques that can add drama and depth to your headshots. Rear curtain sync and high-speed sync are two such techniques that can elevate your flash photography. Rear curtain sync is a fantastic choice for creating a sense of motion. It fires the flash at the end of the exposure, capturing the trail of movement leading up to the still subject, perfect for dynamic, energetic headshots. On the other hand, high-speed sync allows you to use flash with fast shutter speeds above your camera's normal sync speed, which is great for outdoor portraits where you want to open up your aperture for a shallow depth of field without overexposing the shot.

Choosing and Using Flash Modifiers

Modifiers are to flash photographs of what condiments are to a burger—they can make or break your shot. Softboxes, umbrellas, and diffusers are the most common modifiers that help soften the light, making it more flattering for headshots. Softboxes are particularly beloved for their ability to produce a soft, directional light that mimics natural light, ideal for close-up shots where every detail matters. Umbrellas are more accessible to set up and generally create a broader, more diffused light, great for a softer look. Meanwhile, diffusers can be placed directly on your flash to soften its harshness, which is handy for quick, on-the-go shoots.

Experimenting with these modifiers will help you understand how each affects the light and shadow on your subject's face, allowing you to choose the right tool for the desired effect. Whether aiming for a soft, romantic look or a sharp, dramatic feel, using flash and modifiers can significantly enhance your headshots, giving them a professional edge that stands out. So, go ahead, flash that smile—or let your flash bring out the best smiles in your headshots!

Color Gels: Adding Mood and Character

Ah, color gels! These are not just pieces of colored plastic but your ticket to a world where every light can paint a mood set a scene, or tell a story. Think of them as your lighting palette, where each hue can evoke a different emotion or atmosphere. Let's start with a dash of color theory, which is the psychology of how colors affect us. Colors can calm us down, pump us up, or make us feel all sorts of ways without realizing it. For instance, blue can be soothing and professional, red can evoke passion or urgency, and yellow can bring happiness and energy. By understanding these effects, you can use color gels to enhance the emotional impact of your headshots, making them not just pictures but experiences.

Selecting the suitable color gel isn't just about picking your favorite color. It's about matching the color to the message or mood you want the headshot to convey. Are you shooting a corporate headshot? A soft blue might project a vibe of trust and efficiency. Capturing an artist? Magenta or green could amplify their creative, unconventional persona. Once you've chosen your color, it's time to attach the gel to your light source.

This usually involves a gel holder or some clips, but in a pinch, a bit of heat-resistant tape can work, too. Ensure the gel is securely fastened and positioned evenly in front of the light to prevent slipping or uneven color distribution.

Mixing colors can be just as fun as it sounds. You can create custom shades and effects by layering different color gels. For example, a yellow gel with a bit of red can give you a fiery orange, perfect for a bold, energetic headshot. But here's the kicker—you must understand which colors mix well without turning your light into a muddy mess. It's a bit like mixing paints; some combinations are delightful, while others… well, let's say they don't play nice. Experiment with different combinations to see how they blend and complement each other, enhancing the overall mood of your shot.

Let's dive into some practical applications and creative ideas to really get those creative juices flowing. Imagine you're shooting a headshot for a jazz musician. You could use a deep blue gel to bathe them in a cool, moody light reminiscent of a smoky jazz club. Or maybe you're capturing a headshot for a tech entrepreneur. A crisp, green gel could evoke a sense of innovation and energy, aligning perfectly with their forward-thinking persona. These subtle cues, conveyed through color, can make your headshots visually stunning and deeply resonant with the subject's personal or professional brand.

Color gels offer a playground of creativity for photographers. With them, you can manipulate mood, underscore character, and even transform a mundane backdrop into a vivid canvas. Whether subtly enhancing the ambient mood or boldly transforming the light, using color gels in headshot photography opens up a spectrum of possibilities beyond mere illumination. They allow you to paint with light, bringing a dynamic edge to your portraits that sets them apart in the colorful tapestry of visual storytelling. So next time you're setting up for a headshot, consider reaching for a color gel or two—it might just be the splash of color that turns a good headshot into a great one.

The Role of Catchlights in Bringing Headshots to Life

Catchlights are those specks of light that you see twinkling in your subject's eyes, acting as the secret ingredient that makes eyes come alive in photographs. But why fuss over these little glimmers? Well, catchlights add depth and dimension to the eyes, making them appear vibrant and full of life rather than flat and dull. They're like the spark in a conversation that turns a polite "hello" into a captivating dialogue. In headshots, where the connection with the viewer can make or break the photo, ensuring those eyes are expressive and engaging is crucial.

So, how do you go about creating these magical reflections? It starts with your light sources. Your catchlights' shape, size, and intensity are directly influenced by the type of light you use and its positioning. Softboxes, for example, produce a soft and diffused light that creates subtle, usually rectangular catchlights that fill the eyes gently. These are great for a natural, flattering look where you want the subject to appear approachable and friendly. On the other hand, ring lights are fantastic for creating bold, circular catchlights that are often favored in fashion and glamour shots because they give the eyes a bright, arresting look.

Positioning your lights for perfect catchlights is like finding the sweet spot in a game of pin the tail on the donkey, except here, you're aiming for the eyes. A good rule of thumb is to position your leading light at about a 45-degree angle from the direction your subject is facing and slightly above their eye level. This setup not only ensures good overall lighting but also tends to create catchlights at the top of the pupil, where they look most natural and appealing. You can adjust the angle and height of the light to see how it changes the catchlights' shape and intensity, playing around until you find the perfect setup for your particular shoot.

However, sometimes, despite your best efforts, you might run into issues like uneven catchlights or, heaven forbid, no catchlights at all, leaving the eyes looking a bit soulless. Uneven catchlights often occur when one eye is angled differently from the light source, maybe due to the pose or natural face structure. To fix this, you can ask your subject to slightly adjust their head position until the catchlights in both eyes look balanced. If you're not getting any catchlights, your light source is too high, too low, or too far to the side. Try moving it closer and adjusting its height and angle until those little sparks appear in your subject's eyes. Remember, the goal is to mimic how natural light plays in the eyes, so keep tweaking until it looks just right.

Mastering catchlights can dramatically elevate the quality of your headshots, transforming them from simple photographs to portraits that speak to the viewer. By understanding the impact of different light sources and mastering the art of positioning them correctly, you can ensure that every headshot you take captures not just the appearance but the essence of your subject. So next time you're setting up for a shoot, pay special attention to those catchlights—they might be the most minor details in your setup, but their impact on the life and expressiveness of your headshots can be profound.

Multi-Light Setups for Depth and Dimension

In photography, using multiple light sources is like having a full palette of colors when you're painting. It's mixing and matching to create depth, dimension, and drama in your headshots. Let's dive into this multi-dimensional universe where more lights mean more control over how you sculpt your subject's features and set the mood of your portrait.

The Basics of Multi-Light Setups

Think of a multi-light setup as your toolkit for crafting a scene. Each light serves a purpose: key light illuminates your subject, fill light softens shadows, rim light outlines and separates them from the background, and background lights add depth or interest to the scene behind them. The beauty of using multiple lights is that you can precisely control shadows and highlights, creating a three-dimensional look that pops. This method is a game-changer, especially in headshots, where you want your subject to leap off the page (or screen).

Designing a Multi-Light Setup

Planning your lighting setup is like setting the stage for a play. Each light plays a role, and where you place them can dramatically affect the story you're telling. Start with your key light. Typically, it's placed at a 45-degree angle to your subject, slightly above their eye line, to mimic how natural light falls on the face. Next, introduce a fill light on the opposite side, but keep it at about half the intensity of your key light to soften shadows without flattening your image.

Add a rim light behind your subject, opposite the key light. This should be subtle enough to highlight the contours of their hair and shoulders, helping them stand out from the background. Speaking of backgrounds, consider placing a light there too—perhaps with a gel for color or textured with a gobo to add interest. This light shouldn't be too bright; it lifts the background from the darkness and complements the overall composition.

Adjusting Light Ratios for Effect

The light intensity ratio between your key, fill, and rim lights can dramatically alter the mood of your headshots. Want something soft and flattering? Keep your fill light closer in intensity to your key light. Looking for more drama and definition? Increase the contrast by boosting your crucial light and reducing your fill light. These adjustments can help you highlight your subject's best features or create a specific mood that resonates with their personality or the artistic direction of the shoot.

Case Studies and Examples

Let's look at some real-life examples to see these principles in action. Consider a headshot for a corporate executive. You might opt for a conservative setup with soft, even lighting here. Key and fill lights are balanced to minimize shadows, and a gentle rim light ensures they pop against a muted background. The mood is professional and approachable, perfect for a LinkedIn profile or company website.

Now, imagine a jazz musician's headshot. Here, dial up the drama. Increase the intensity of the key light, pull back the fill light to deepen the shadows, and use a colored gel on the background light to echo the mood of a smoky jazz bar. The result is a headshot with character and depth that tells a story at a glance.

By mastering multi-light setups, you're not just taking pictures but crafting images with intention. You have the power to control every aspect of how your subject is perceived, from their best physical features to the deeper nuances of their personality. This control turns a standard headshot into a compelling portrait that captures and holds attention.

As we wrap up this exploration of multi-light setups, remember that the key to success lies in experimentation and adaptation. Each subject is unique, and how you light them should be, too. Use these tools to bring out their best and create headshots that are not only technically proficient but also emotionally resonant. Armed with these lighting strategies, you're ready to move on and explore even more creative dimensions in headshot photography.

Chapter 3: The Human Element: Directing and Posing

Picture this: you've set up the perfect studio, the lighting is impeccable, and your camera is just itching to snap that million-dollar shot, but there's just one hiccup – your subject steps in, and suddenly, the room feels as chilly as a winter's day in Siberia. Uh-oh, it's the classic case of first-shoot jitters! Fear not, because this chapter is about breaking the ice and turning that nervous energy into creative synergy. After all, a headshot is only as good as the comfort and confidence exuding from your subject.

Breaking the Ice: First Steps in Subject Interaction

Creating a Welcoming Environment

First impressions are like a good espresso – solid and impactful. So, let's make your studio feel like the next best thing to a cozy café where everyone wants to hang out. You can start by ensuring the temperature is just right.

Too cold, and your subject might as well be posing for a snowman catalog; too hot, and everyone's sweating more than in a sauna. Next, consider your lighting – soft, warm lights can make your studio feel inviting rather than a high-stakes interrogation room.

A neat trick is to have some soft background music playing. Choose tunes that are calming or cheerful to help soothe nerves. Think of it as the background soundtrack of your subject's movie– something that subtly lifts the mood without overpowering the scene. And hey, why not offer a beverage? A cup of coffee or a glass of water can make your subject feel cared for and attended to. These little gestures say, "Welcome, let's make something beautiful together."

Personal Introductions and Rapport Building

Now, with the stage set, it's showtime – and by showtime, I mean 'get-to-know-you' time. Before asking your subject to pose, engage them in chit-chat. Introduce yourself with a warm smile, offer a handshake or an elbow bump, and thank them for coming. Share a bit about your experience and what excited you about this shoot. Then, invite them to tell you about themselves. This isn't just small talk; it's your opportunity to pick up on details that can help personalize their session later. Maybe they mention a hobby or a passion that you can reference to lighten the mood or draw a genuine smile during the shoot.

Understanding Your Subject's Vision

Every headshot is a story, and your subject is the protagonist. Take the time to understand the chapter they want to tell through this photo. Is this headshot for a corporate website, a creative portfolio, or personal branding? Each purpose might dictate a different style or expression. Open up this dialogue by asking questions like, "What adjectives would you want someone to use when they see this photo?" or "Is there a headshot you've seen and loved that you want to emulate in some way?" This conversation aligns your artistic direction and makes your subjects feel they are co-creators in the process, which can significantly boost their investment and enthusiasm for the session.

Pre-shoot Questionnaire

Consider using a pre-shoot questionnaire to make your life a tad easier and these discussions more fruitful. This handy tool can help you gather important details about your subject's expectations, preferences, and even apprehensions before they enter the studio. Ask them to fill it out a day or two before the session. Include questions about their goals for the shoot, any particular styles they like, colors that make them feel confident, or even parts of their appearance they are susceptible to. This not only primes them for the shoot but also gives you a head start on tailoring the session to meet their vision.

When you're ready to start shooting, you and your subject will feel like a team prepared to tackle this creative challenge together. With the ice properly broken and a warm rapport established, those initial jitters will transform into collaborative energy, paving the way for a session where every click of the shutter counts. And who knows? By the end of it, you have turned a nervous subject into a photo-session enthusiast, eager to come back for more.

Posing Techniques for Flattering Headshots

When it comes to posing, think of yourself as a photographer and a sculptor, where your medium isn't marble or clay but space, light, and human posture. The right pose can elevate a headshot from simple to stunning, transforming how the subject is perceived by its audience. So, let's roll up our sleeves and get into the nitty-gritty of posing techniques that flatter, intrigue, and tell a story.

Fundamentals of Flattering Poses

The basics of a good pose hinge on several fundamental principles: posture, angles, and the use of space. A straight posture, for instance, conveys confidence and professionalism, ideal for corporate headshots. However, a slight tilt of the head or a playful shift in weight can inject a bit of personality and motion, making the shot feel more dynamic and relatable. It's all about the angles – no, not your Instagram filters – but the physical angles formed by the limbs and the body. For instance, angling the shoulders slightly towards the camera can create a slimming effect, while positioning the hands in a thoughtful manner near the face can draw attention to the subject's expression, adding layers of subtlety to the narrative you're capturing.

Angles are your secret weapon; they can dramatically affect the mood and impact of a headshot. A lower angle can make your subject appear more imposing or heroic, perfect for an author's portrait on a book cover. Conversely, a higher angle can be more flattering and approachable, suitable for a friendly social media profile pic. It's all about how you want the viewer to perceive the person in the shot.

Pose Variations for Different Body Types

Some people come in different shapes and sizes, and that's where your creativity as a photographer comes into play. Tailoring poses to suit various body types is crucial in highlighting each subject's best features. For someone with a taller frame, let them sit down to create a more intimate and inviting scene. For fuller figures, use poses that create angles with their arms and legs to craft a balanced and beautiful composition. Encourage them to shift their weight to one leg or use their hands to create space between their arms and torso, which can result in a more styled and graceful image.

Remember, the goal here is to make every subject feel like the best version of themselves in front of your lens. This isn't just about physical appearances—it's about making them see how awesome they look through your eyes or lens.

Dynamic vs. Static Poses

The choice between a dynamic and a static pose can set the tone of the headshot. Static poses, where the subject is calm and composed, often looking directly at the camera, are fantastic for traditional, formal shots focusing squarely on the person's face and expression. These are your go-to for professional LinkedIn images or corporate websites.

Dynamic poses, where the subject might be captured in motion or just about to move, inject life and energy into the shot. These are great for creative professionals, artists, or performers, where a sense of movement can hint at their dynamic capabilities or vibrant personalities. Capturing a laugh, a gesture, or an off-the-cuff glance can make the headshot more personal and engaging.

Using Props for Natural Poses

Props can be a fantastic way to help subjects relax and engage more naturally with the camera. The right prop can add context to the shot, reflect the subject's personality, or give their hands something to do. A writer might hold a book, a musician their instrument, or a chef a rolling pin. These items add interest to the composition and help tell the subject's story more effectively.

Moreover, props can help subjects feel less self-conscious as they'll partly focus on the object, leading to more relaxed and genuine expressions. The key is to ensure the prop complements the shot and doesn't distract from the subject. It should feel like an extension of their personality, not a random addition.

By integrating these techniques into your headshot sessions, you're not just taking photos but crafting portraits that speak volumes. Each pose, each angle, and each prop works together to create a snapshot that is not only visually appealing but also rich in narrative, perfectly tailored to each individual who steps in front of your camera. So, play with these techniques, and watch your headshots transform from simple pictures to stories told in light, posture, and expression.

Communicating with Non-Models for Authentic Expressions

When you aim to capture the genuine essence of a person not used to flashing cameras and fashion poses, the dance between director and subject becomes subtly complex. It's like guiding someone through a maze; you know the way, but you need them to trust you enough to follow your lead. The magic in capturing authentic expressions lies in commanding and gently steering the session to allow those natural, unguarded moments to shine through.

Directing Without Dictating

Imagine you're helping a friend learn a dance move. You wouldn't just bark orders; you'd demonstrate, give feedback, and maybe even dance with them. This approach transforms nervous energy into collaborative play in photography, especially with non-models. Start by explaining the purpose of each pose or expression in terms of the result. For instance, you might say, "Tilt your head slightly to capture the light—it will highlight your eyes and give them that spark." This way, you share the 'why' behind your directions, which helps demystify the process and engage your subject more deeply.

Encourage your subjects by showing them some of the shots as you go. A quick peek at the camera screen can boost their confidence and help them visualize what works. It's about creating an environment where they feel safe to experiment and see themselves as partners in the creative process. Remember, the goal here is to guide, not govern. Your gentle suggestions and shared control can lead to stunningly sincere portraits that might surprise both of you.

Finding the Subject's Best Angles

Every face tells a story, and every story has its perfect angle. The trick is to find it quickly and use it effectively. Start by observing your subjects as they talk or move naturally. People often reveal their best angles spontaneously. For example, someone might naturally turn their head to one side in a way that perfectly catches the light and softens their features. Once you spot these moments, encourage your subject to hold or return to that pose.

A good technique is to have your subject slowly rotate their head from left to right and take a few quick shots at various angles. Review these shots together and point out which angles are most flattering. This not only helps you identify the best perspectives but also involves your subject in the decision-making process, making them more invested and likely to relax into those angles during the shoot.

Encouraging Spontaneous Expressions

The best expressions are never forced; they're coaxed into existence with a mix of tact and timing. Engage your subject in light conversation while you shoot—ask about their passions, happiest memories, or even what they had for breakfast. These conversations can elicit a range of genuine emotions, from thoughtful smiles to bursts of laughter, providing you with a spectrum of expressions to capture.

Another fun method is to use action prompts. For instance, ask them to laugh at your worst joke or show you their reaction to finding $20 in an old coat. These actions can break the stiffness and surface sparkling moments of genuine emotion. Always be ready to snap these fleeting expressions, often making for the most memorable and impactful images.

Dealing with Camera Shyness

Camera shyness is like a stubborn clam. But with patience and the right approach, you can coax it open to reveal the pearl inside. Start by acknowledging their nervousness and reassure them that it's perfectly normal. A little empathy goes a long way. Practice poses and expressions before you even pick up the camera. Review a few poses, mirror them, and discuss what feels natural. This rehearsal can ease the tension, making the actual shoot feel more like a continuation of the practice rather than a spotlight moment.

Sometimes, simply redirecting their focus helps. Ask them to look at a point slightly above or to the side of the lens. This can reduce the intimidation of direct eye contact with the camera, often resulting in a more relaxed and natural look.

Also, keep talking them through the process, letting them know when they nail a pose or expression. This continuous feedback loop keeps the session lively and diminishes the daunting feeling of being scrutinized through the lens.

By weaving these strategies into your interactions, you transform the camera from a barrier into a bridge, connecting you and your subject in the pursuit of capturing the authentic self. It's about making the process as enjoyable and engaging as the results. After all, photography is not just about seeing; it's about feeling, and the more comfortable and connected your subject feels, the more their inner self will shine through in the final portrait.

The Power of Micro-Expressions in Headshot Photography

Identifying Micro-Expressions

Let's chat about those fleeting flashes of feelings that flit across someone's face faster than a New York minute—micro-expressions. These subtle, often subconscious, emotional signals zip by in less than half a second. Imagine capturing the spark of joy in someone's eyes as they recall a fond memory or the quick furrow of a brow in contemplative thought. These tiny expressions can tell a big part of the story, often conveying more sincerity and emotion than a staged smile ever could.

Understanding how to spot and capture these micro-moments can elevate your headshot photography from good to down-right compelling. It starts with keen observation. Before you even pick up your camera, spend time with your subject, chatting and observing the natural play of expressions as they talk about their interests or recount a recent event. Notice the quick changes in their facial expressions—these are your gold mines. Each micro-expression reflects a genuine emotion, and capturing these can add a layer of depth and authenticity to your headshots that staged poses might not communicate.

Timing and Anticipation

Now, capturing these micro-expressions requires a bit of psychic ability—okay, not really, but you do need to master the art of anticipation. It's about predicting when these expressions might occur and being ready at just the right moment. This skill is akin to a wildlife photographer waiting for that perfect shot when the lion roars; it's all about patience and readiness.

Keep your camera poised and observe your subject during the conversation. Watch for patterns in their expressions— people often show a particular micro-expression when they talk about specific topics. For instance, someone might light up with a subtle sparkle in their eyes every time they mention their passion project. Once you identify these triggers, you can guide the conversation around topics that might elicit those expressions. This approach requires a delicate balance—you want to encourage these moments to surface naturally, without making the subject feel like they're under a microscope.

Encouraging a Range of Emotions

To truly capture the essence of your subject, encourage a spectrum of emotions during the shoot. This doesn't mean turning the session into an emotional rollercoaster but rather gently guiding your subject through a variety of emotional states. It could be as simple as asking them to recall a proud moment, describe a relaxing weekend, or imagine achieving a long-term goal.

As you engage in these conversations, keep the atmosphere light and supportive. It's crucial that your subject feels safe and understood, as the more comfortable they are, the more likely they are to express genuine emotions. Remember, every subtle shift in emotion can bring about a change in expression, and these are the moments you want to capture. Your ability to read the room and adapt your conversation can make all the difference in the range and authenticity of the expressions you photograph.

Analyzing Expressions in Real Time

Becoming adept at analyzing expressions in real time is like developing a superpower. It allows you to see beyond the obvious and capture the essence of your subject's personality. Keep your eyes peeled for the nuances—the slight raise of an eyebrow, a twitch at the corner of the mouth, a fleeting look of contemplation. These are the details that add character to a headshot.

Continuously assess the expressions you're capturing and adjust your approach accordingly. If you notice that specific topics bring more relaxed and open expressions, steer the conversation in that direction. Conversely, if some topics cause your subject to close off, it's wise to tread lightly or shift gears. Responding to these real-time cues helps capture the best possible shots and ensures your subject has a positive and enjoyable experience.

By integrating these techniques into your workflow, you open up a world where every click of the shutter has the potential to reveal a layer of the human soul. Micro-expressions, when caught, are like secret whispers of the heart captured in pixel and print, offering a glimpse into the unguarded self. As you refine your ability to spot, anticipate, and capture these fleeting expressions, your portfolio will grow in quantity and storytelling depth, making your headshots not just pictures, but portraits of raw, unedited humanity.

Handling Nervous or Uncooperative Subjects

So, you've got your camera ready, and your studio is set, but there's a hiccup: your subject could be sweating bullets, or maybe they're about as cooperative as a cat in a bath. No worries! Whether pre-shoot jitters or a touch of defiance, there are foolproof ways to turn the tide and make your photo session a win-win. Remember, every great director knows how to turn a bit of on-set drama into a blockbuster finale.

Strategies for Nervous Subjects

Let's start with those butterflies in the stomach. It's normal for folks to feel like they're about to give a speech rather than smile for the camera. First off, normalize those nerves. Let them know it's perfectly okay to feel a bit anxious. Sometimes, just acknowledging the elephant in the room can make it much less intimidating. Next up, breathing exercises can be a game-changer. Guide them through a simple routine: breathe in slowly through the nose, hold for a second, and exhale through the mouth. Repeat a few times. It's incredible how a little oxygen can turn tension into tranquility.

But hey, not all fixes need to be so serene. Sometimes, just breaking the routine helps. If you sense the tension isn't easing, suggest a quick break. Step away from the studio for a couple of minutes. Chat about this and that—maybe the latest movie or some funky new restaurant. This casual banter can work wonders, making the studio feel less like a spotlight and more like a conversation space. When you return, you'll often find those nerves have packed up and left.

Turning Resistance into Collaboration

Now, for the spirited souls who might see a camera and think it's a duel at dawn rather than a friendly shoot. Here's where your interpersonal magic comes into play. Start by setting the stage for collaboration, not confrontation. Explain your process clearly—what you're going to do and why. This transparency removes the unknown and helps establish trust.

If you hit a bump, like a pose they detest or a style they scoff at, don't push back with authority. Instead, lean in with empathy. Ask what they don't like about it and what they might prefer instead. Sometimes, just feeling heard can soften resistance. Turn their feedback into action. Try their idea, then gently guide them back to what you know works best. Often, they'll be more open to suggestions once they see you're genuinely trying to align with their preferences.

Adapting Your Approach

Flexibility is your best friend when managing a range of personalities and comfort levels. Some folks might revel in rapid-fire poses and constant changes, while others may need more time to warm up to each camera click. Read their cues. If someone seems overwhelmed by too many directions, slow it down. Focus on one adjustment at a time. Conversely, if someone gets bored or distracted, it might be time to speed things up or introduce a new prop or background to re-engage them.

Remember, there's no one-size-fits-all approach to directing a shoot. Each subject is unique, and your ability to adapt not only makes for smoother sessions but also better portraits. After all, a relaxed subject who feels in sync with their photographer is more likely to shine in front of the camera.

Building Trust Through Transparency

Trust is the secret sauce in the recipe for a successful shoot. And how do you whip up this trust? Start by being transparent about the process. Show them photos during the shoot, discuss what you think works, and invite their input. This peek behind the curtain can be incredibly reassuring, making the subject feel they're part of the creation process, not just the subject of it.

Moreover, explain why you're choosing specific settings or poses. For instance, "I'm using a wider aperture now because it makes your eyes stand out," or "This pose brings out the great lines of your jaw." Understanding the why behind your decisions can change your perspective from feeling like a prop to being an active participant in a creative endeavor.

In the dance of photography, leading gracefully means knowing when to guide and when to follow subtly. By employing these strategies, you transform potential standoff moments into opportunities for creative collaboration. Each session then becomes not just about capturing a great photo, but about crafting a positive experience that they'll remember just as fondly as they do the portraits you create together.

Cultivating a Session Atmosphere for Great Performances

Imagine stepping into a studio where the air is just buzzing with the right kind of energy—where every note of music and every piece of feedback builds up to a crescendo of creativity. That's the dream, right? Well, it's totally achievable. It all starts with setting the perfect mood and maintaining an energy that keeps both you and your subject tuned in and jazzed up for the entire session. So, let's turn up the dial to create an atmosphere that inspires and transforms any session into a performance worth remembering.

Music and Mood

Let's talk tunes. Music isn't just background noise; it's a powerful mood enhancer. Think about how a certain beat can lift your spirit or how a particular melody can calm your nerves. In a photography session, the choice of music can set the tone for the entire shoot. Tailor your playlist to fit the vibe you're aiming for. Some light acoustic tracks will do the trick if you're going for a laid-back, approachable look. Shooting something more high-energy? Perhaps some upbeat pop or funky jazz would be more fitting. But here's the kicker: always consider your subject's music preference. Ask them beforehand what tunes make them feel good or keep them energized. This not only makes them more comfortable but also personalizes the session, making them feel genuinely part of the creative process. Music becomes a bridge, connecting you through shared vibes and bopping heads.

Maintaining Energy and Focus

Keeping the energy up doesn't require you to morph into a cheerleader, but a little enthusiasm never hurts! It's more about maintaining a lively pace and engaging in the process. Show excitement about the shots you're capturing. Your energy is contagious, and when your subjects see you getting excited, they'll feed off that vibe and bring their A-game. But balance is critical. Keep an eye on your subject's energy levels. If you sense a dip— maybe they're getting tired or overwhelmed— take it as your cue to switch things up. Suggest a quick break, change the backdrop, or flip to a new music track. These little refreshers can prevent fatigue and keep the session dynamic and productive.

Creating a Collaborative Environment

Photography, especially portraits, is an art of collaboration. It's not just about you directing every pose but about creating a space where your subjects feel they can contribute their ideas and feedback. Encourage them to suggest adjustments or share thoughts on what feels natural. This inclusion makes the session more of a team effort and less about following orders. A simple "What do you think about this pose?" or "Feel free to adjust if that feels awkward" can make all the difference. It shows respect for their comfort and input, boosting their confidence and fostering a partnership that can lead to more authentic and personalized shots.

Handling Feedback Positively

Feedback is a two-way street. It's about giving and receiving comments in a way that uplifts and improves the session. When you provide feedback, frame it positively. Instead of saying, "Don't slouch," try, "I love how confident you look when you stand tall." This positive spin encourages rather than criticizes, making the subject feel good about making adjustments. On the flip side, be open to receiving feedback. If a subject isn't keen on a particular pose or their expression in a preview, don't brush it off. Listen, adjust, and thank them for their input. This open dialogue enhances the photos and ensures they leave the session feeling heard and respected, qualities that define a truly great photographer-client relationship.

By weaving these elements into your sessions, you create more than just stunning photos; you craft memorable experiences that resonate with your subjects. Each session becomes a symphony of interactions, where the music sets the tempo, your energy conducts the rhythm, collaboration harmonizes the melody, and positive feedback rings out the final notes. This is where great performances are born, not just in the photos captured but in the very atmosphere of your studio. So, let's make every shutter click a note in this beautiful composition we call portrait photography.

Gender Considerations in Posing and Direction

Understanding the nuances of gender can be as pivotal as knowing your way around a camera when stepping into the realm of headshot photography. It's about more than just asking someone to smile and snap a picture; it's about creating an environment and crafting poses that respect individual comfort while challenging societal perceptions. Each session is a delicate balance of being mindful of these aspects while striving to portray each person authentically and powerfully.

Navigating gender nuances begins with an open dialogue about how each subject envisions themselves in their headshot. This conversation is crucial as it sets the stage for a shoot where subjects feel seen and respected. For instance, while some men might prefer more traditionally masculine poses that emphasize strength and solidity, others might opt for softer, more fluid poses that express different aspects of their personality. Similarly, women might be looking for poses that project confidence and professionalism, countering the often softer portrayals in media. In these discussions, it's essential to steer clear of gender-based assumptions. Each person brings a unique blend of traits and preferences that should guide how you direct them rather than relying on outdated stereotypes.

Avoiding stereotypes in posing and expression is not just about being politically correct; it's about breaking molds and celebrating individuality. Stereotypical poses—like a man with crossed arms looking stern or a woman gently smiling —can sometimes undermine the subject's multi-dimensional traits. Instead, consider poses that enhance their persona. For a CEO, regardless of gender, you might direct them to lean slightly forward, hands on a table, looking up with a determined expression. This pose exudes leadership and decisiveness. For creative professionals, having them look away from the camera, lost in thought, can add an element of introspection and creativity, universally appealing traits.

Empowering your subjects through poses is a powerful way to ensure they are satisfied with their headshots and challenge traditional perceptions. For instance, using poses that show-case a subject's tattoos or unique fashion sense can be a form of empowerment, allowing them to display aspects of their identity that they cherish proudly. Encourage poses that make them feel strong, confident, and authentic. This could be as simple as adjusting how they stand or the placement of their hands; minor tweaks can make a big difference in how they perceive themselves in the final product.

Sensitive communication is the golden thread that ties all these elements together. It's about more than just giving directions; it's about how you make your subjects feel during the shoot. Use language that is inclusive and affirming, and be open to feedback. If a pose or direction seems to make them uncomfortable, be quick to adapt and suggest an alternative. Show that you are attentive to their needs and respect their boundaries. This kind of sensitive interaction ensures that they feel comfortable and respected and helps capture genuine expressions that are true to who they are.

Every headshot session is a collaborative effort to produce a stunning photograph and make a statement about identity and self-expression. By being mindful of gender nuances, avoiding stereotypes, empowering subjects, and communicating sensitively, you create more than just a picture. You craft an experience that celebrates and respects the unique individuals who step before your lens, capturing their true essence in a way that resonates with them personally and professionally.

Capturing the Essence of Your Subject: Beyond the Pose

Capturing the essence of your subject goes beyond asking them to hold a smile and click away. It's like being a detective of personality, where each shot aims to unveil a part of the subject's story that they might not even see daily. Start by peering beyond the physical pose. A good pose is just the beginning; the magic happens when you manage to capture those in-between moments when the subject's guard is down and their genuine self shimmers through. This requires you to be observant, patient, and ready to catch that spark of authenticity.

Encouraging photographers to look beyond the pose means coaching them to see each subject as a unique narrative waiting to be told. For instance, during the shoot, pay close attention to how your subject reacts to different topics of conversation. A nostalgic smile as they mention a childhood memory, a spark in their eyes when they talk about a passion project, or a slight frown when discussing a challenge—they all tell parts of their story that a mere pose cannot convey. Capturing these micro-reactions involves your skills behind the camera and your ability to connect on a human level. It's about making the camera invisible and creating a space where the subject feels free to express their genuine emotions.

Moreover, engaging subjects in meaningful conversation is pivotal in this process. It's not just small talk; it's strategic communication designed to reveal the subject's character. Begin by asking open-ended questions that invite them to share stories, not just answers. Questions like, "What's something you're proud of?" or "Tell me about a place that feels like home" can elicit responses that bring out heartfelt expressions and gestures. Listen actively and show genuine interest. This helps build a connection and makes the subject feel valued, often leading to more open and natural interactions in front of the lens.

The environment and context in which you shoot can also significantly impact how well you capture the essence of your subject. Every element in the background, the lighting, and even the colors can contribute to the story you're trying to tell. For example, shooting a professional headshot in a cluttered, dimly lit room might distract from the subject's professionalism. Conversely, a well-organized, brightly lit setting can enhance their authoritative presence. Similarly, for more artistic or casual portraits, choosing an environment that resonates with the subject's style— like a graffiti-filled alley for a musician or a lush green park for a nature lover— can add meaning to the photograph. The key is to align the setting with the narrative you and the subject aim to convey, making the environment a complementary element to the portrait's story.

Collaboration with the subject throughout the process is crucial for authentic representation in their headshot. This partnership begins when they enter the studio or chosen venue. Maintain a dialogue that keeps them involved in every decision— from the choice of background to the selection of props and the posing style. Please encourage them to suggest changes or voice their preferences. This collaborative approach ensures that the headshots reflect their true persona and boosts their confidence in the outcome. It transforms the shoot from a mere session into a shared creative journey, where the subject actively participates in crafting their image. This level of involvement can significantly enhance the authenticity of the photographs, capturing not just a person's look but their essence— making every headshot a true reflection of the individual.

By incorporating these strategies into your workflow, you create more than just beautiful images; you create stories.

Each photograph becomes a canvas where the subject's personality, environment, and photographic skill interplay to produce something unique and personal. So, remember, next time you pick up your camera for a headshot, you're not just capturing faces; you're capturing stories, emotions, and the unseen beauty of individuality.

Feedback Loop: The Key to Effective Directing

Imagine you're cooking a gourmet meal. You taste a sauce, tweak it, get a second opinion, adjust again—this feedback cycle ensures that your final dish is nothing short of mouth-watering. Similarly, in photography, establishing a robust feedback loop during your shoots can turn those initial test shots into stunning, gallery-worthy headshots. Feedback, when done right, acts like a compass, guiding you and your subject toward the best possible outcomes, bite by bite, or in our case, click by click.

Immediate Feedback for Improvement

Let's talk about the magic of instant feedback. Say you're in the middle of a shoot, and you just captured a pose. Instead of moving on, please take a moment to review it with your subject. This isn't about nitpicking but celebrating what's working and adjusting what isn't. Maybe a slight chin tilt or a lower-hand position could transform a good shot into a great one. By discussing these tweaks on the spot, you refine the shots and educate your subject on what poses and expressions bring out their best. This immediate, constructive dialogue helps build their confidence and understanding of the process, making them more active participants in creating their headshots. Plus, it saves you from a mountain of post-shoot editing because it's easier to get it right in the camera than to play Wizard in Photoshop later.

Encouraging Subject Self-Feedback

While your expert eye is invaluable, empowering your subjects to assess and comment on their images can be incredibly fruitful. After taking a few shots, invite your subject to review them. Ask open-ended questions like, "What do you think about this expression?" or "How do you feel about your pose here?" This isn't just about getting them 'okay' on the shots but encouraging a deeper engagement with their portrayal. Often, subjects see things about themselves that you might overlook, and their input can lead to adjustments that make the images more authentic and personal. Plus, this practice helps demystify the photographic process, making it less about the mystery behind the lens and more about shared storytelling.

Post-Shoot Review for Learning

The learning isn't over after the lights are off and the camera is packed away. Scheduling a post-shoot review can be incredibly beneficial, especially if you're building a long-term relationship with your subject or their brand. This can be as informal as a follow-up call or a sit-down meeting over coffee. Go through the images together and discuss what worked and could be improved. This isn't just about critique but reflection and learning. What angles, lighting, or expressions captured their essence best? What didn't translate as well as expected? These insights are gold, helping you prepare better for future shoots and refine your collaborative process.

Ongoing Feedback for Long-Term Relationships

In photography, as in life, the best relationships are built on ongoing, open dialogue. Whether it's regular check-ins with repeat clients or an annual review session, keep the lines of communication open. This ongoing feedback loop helps you stay aligned with your subjects' evolving styles, needs, and objectives. It ensures that your services grow with their personal or professional branding, keeping your collaborations fresh and relevant. Plus, this sustained engagement turns clients into long-term partners and, often, champions of your work in their networks.

You transform each shoot from a mere transaction to a dynamic and educational experience by weaving these feedback strategies into your directing process. It's about building a cycle of continuous improvement, where each round of feedback sharpens your skills and deepens the trust between you and your subjects. So, embrace the power of feedback—it's your secret ingredient to meeting and exceeding expectations, one shoot at a time.

As we wrap up this chapter on the human element in photography, remember that each interaction, every piece of feedback, and every adjustment is a step towards perfecting your craft and strengthening your relationships. The insights gained here are not just about improving single images but about enriching your overall approach to photography, ensuring that each session you direct is more intuitive, collaborative, and successful than the last. So keep this feedback loop spinning because in photography, like gourmet cooking, the best results come from taste, tweak, and repeat.

In our next chapter, we'll shift our focus from the shooting process to what happens after the art and science of post-processing. It's where the raw materials of your shoot meet the polish and precision of your artistic vision, turning good shots into great ones. So, ready your editing tools— it's time to dive into the pixels and details that elevate your headshots from captured to beautifully crafted.

Chapter 4: Post-Processing and Retouching

Picture this: you've just wrapped up a fabulous photo shoot and are excited as you import the day's haul into your computer. Suddenly, you're not just a photographer— you're a wizard, ready to weave some post-processing magic! But before you start zapping pixels, let's demystify the mystical world of post-processing software, where your raw images transform into polished gems.

Introduction to Post-Processing Software

Navigating Software Options

Diving into the sea of post-processing software can be as daunting as choosing a doughnut at a bakery—so many tempting options, but which is the right pick for your sweet tooth? Let's narrow down the choices to a few giants in headshot retouching: Adobe Photoshop, Lightroom, and Capture One.

Photoshop, the granddaddy of image editing, offers unparalleled tools and features that cater to both the creative and the meticulous. Lightroom, Photoshop's younger sibling, simplifies workflow and file management, making it a favorite for photographers needing efficiency and quality. Then there's Capture One, known for its superior color handling and detailed image quality, a hit among those who want to dive deep into the nitty-gritty of pixel perfection. Each software has its strengths, and the best fit depends on your specific needs— Photoshop for the detail-oriented retoucher, Lightroom for the fast-paced editor, and Capture One for the color perfectionist.

Understanding the Interface

Now, let's talk about staying aware of the digital jungle of panels, tools, and menus. Starting with Photoshop: imagine it as your artist's studio. Here, your tools are on one side (the toolbox), your canvas is in the middle (the workspace), and your color palettes and brushes are on the other side (the panels). Lightroom simplifies this: think of it as your photo album, where everything from importing to editing to exporting is done in a streamlined, module-based layout. With its customizable interface, Capture One allows you to set up your workspace as you like— whether you're left-handed, right-handed, or a no-hands automated wizard using presets! Familiarizing yourself with these interfaces is like learning where everything is in your new apartment— the sooner you know, the quicker you feel at home.

Developing a Workflow

Creating a consistent workflow is like setting up a good morning routine— ensuring you start on the right foot daily. Post-processing means establishing a series of steps you follow with each image, ensuring efficiency and consistency in your edits. Start by culling your images to select the best shots. Next, adjust your basic settings (exposure, contrast, color balance) for a uniform look. Then, dive into more detailed edits like skin retouching and eye enhancement. Finally, add your creative touches like filters or effects before preparing the images for export. This workflow isn't just about keeping you organized; it's about making the post-processing phase a streamlined, stress-free experience where creativity remains the front-runner.

Software Tutorials and Resources

Feeling overwhelmed? Don't worry; there's a treasure trove of learning resources out there. For Photoshop and Lightroom, Adobe offers a comprehensive library of tutorials that cover everything from basic adjustments to advanced manipulation. Capture One also provides detailed guides and webinars tailored to its unique tools and features. Additionally, platforms like YouTube are goldmines of knowledge, with channels dedicated to photography and retouching. Follow a few, and you'll be mastering curves and masks like a pro in no time. Remember, the goal isn't just to learn how to use the software but to understand how to make it work for you, enhancing your unique style and workflow.

As you embark on this post-processing adventure, remember that the software is merely a tool—your creative vision will truly bring those pixels to life. So, harness these digital brushes and chisels, and let's turn those raw captures into masterpieces that look great and capture the essence of your artistic intent. And with that, let's leap into the finer points of basic retouching, where we'll smooth, enhance, and polish your way to stunning headshots that will turn heads.

Basic Retouching: Skin, Eyes, and Hair

Ah, the world of basic retouching—where the good becomes extraordinary, and the 'meh' photos transform into 'wow' portraits. Let's roll up our digital sleeves and dive into the techniques to help you polish up those headshots like a pro, focusing on three key areas: skin, eyes, and hair. These elements are critical in portrait photography because they draw the most attention in a headshot. Done right, they can elevate your photo; done wrong, well, let's make sure we do it right, shall we?

Skin Smoothing Techniques

Starting with the skin, think of it as the canvas of your portrait. You want it to look flawless but not plastic. Over-smoothed skin is a common faux pas that can leave your subject looking more like a wax figure than a natural person. To avoid this, embrace the texture. Yes, you heard that right. The skin has texture, and preserving it is vital to maintaining a natural look. Tools like the Healing Brush and Clone Stamp in Photoshop are perfect. Use them to tap away at blemishes or uneven spots gently. Think of it as spot-cleaning a fancy suit; you're not scrubbing the whole thing, just tidying up where necessary.

Next, play around with the High Pass filter and a layer mask for a smooth but textured appearance. This method allows you to apply smoothing only where you need it, like on uneven skin tones or shadows, without affecting the sharp areas that give the face its character. Adjust the opacity to keep it accurate—your subject shouldn't look like they've been dipped in porcelain glaze!

Enhancing Eyes

Moving on to the windows of the soul—the eyes. They're often the focal point of any headshot, and getting them just right can really make your photo pop. Start with the whites. Yes, even the whites of the eyes need a bit of TLC. Lighten them slightly with a non-destructive Dodge tool, but remember, slight is the keyword here. You're aiming for bright and alert, not stormtrooper helmets.

Enhance the irises' natural color with a Hue/Saturation adjustment layer. Boost the saturation for a bit of intensity, but let's keep them looking like they belong on Earth, shall we? To add some sparkle, catchlights can be enhanced or even said if they're not pronounced. Use a soft white brush on a new layer, set to Overlay, and tap a small dot where the light naturally hits. This little twinkle adds life to the eyes, making your subject look lively and sharp.

Hair Retouching Tips

Now, let's tame those locks. Hair can be tricky, with flyaways and frizz often ruining an otherwise perfect shot. Start using the Healing Brush to zap away stray hairs that cross the face or outline. Be meticulous but conservative; overdoing it can make the hairline look unnaturally clean. To add shine and depth, dodge and burn strategically. Darken the shadows and lighten the highlights to give hair a lustrous, healthy appearance. This step is like adding a bit of hairspray—not too much, just enough to make it look stylish and put together.

For color, if the hair looks washed out or uneven, a quick sweep of color balance or selective color adjustment can enrich the natural tones. Think of it as giving your subject a virtual salon visit—they come out looking refreshed and vibrant, ready for their close-up.

Avoiding Common Retouching Mistakes

Lastly, let's touch on what not to do. Common pitfalls in retouching can make your job harder and the results less appealing. Avoid going overboard with any of the tools. Subtlety is your best friend in retouching. Keep checking your before and after to ensure you have stayed within the realm of over-editing. Another tip is to keep your workflow non-destructive. Use layers and adjustment layers so you can always go back and tweak without starting over. This approach saves time and preserves your sanity.

Remember, the goal of retouching is to enhance, not to overshadow. You're looking to highlight the best features of your subjects, not paint a new face on them. Keep it real, keep it subtle, and above all, keep it respectful to the natural beauty of your subject. With these tips and techniques, you're well on your way to mastering the art of basic retouching, turning those good shots into great portraits that look professional, polished, and profoundly striking. Now, let's carry these polished portraits into advanced techniques, where we fine-tune our skills and make those details sing.

Advanced Retouching Techniques: Beyond the Basics

When you've mastered the basics of retouching and are ready to flex your editing muscles a bit more, it's time to step into the arena of advanced techniques. Here, we're not just tweaking; we're transforming and fine-tuning to create depth, detail, and drama in ways that basic edits can't touch. Let's peel back the curtain on more sophisticated tricks that can take your headshots from "nice" to "Whoa, tell me more!"

Dodging and Burning for Depth

First up on our tour of advanced techniques is the age-old art of dodging and burning. This isn't just about making things lighter or darker; it's about sculpting light and shadow to add a three-dimensional quality to your images that pulls viewers in. Picture this: you're working on a headshot, and while it's technically acceptable, itl acks a specific 'pop.'By selectively darkening some areas (burning) and lightening others (dodging), you can highlight facial contours, enhance muscle structure, or even simulate a more flattering light scenario.

Think of it as applying makeup with light. You might use burning to deepen the shadows under the cheekbones and along the jawline, adding a chiseled strength to the face. Conversely, dodging can bring out the eyes by subtly lightening the irises and adding a touch of brightness to the under-eye area, reducing darkness and puffiness. The key here is subtlety; overdo it, and you risk venturing into uncanny valley territory where things look too perfect to be real. A gentle touch enhances features without making them look artificial.

Frequency Separation for Detailed Skin Retouching

Moving on, let's talk about frequency separation. This technique sounds like something from a sci-fi movie, but it's a game-changer for retouchers. Frequency separation splits your image into two layers: one that holds the textures (high frequency) and one that has the tones and colors (low frequency). Why does this matter? Because it allows you to work on fine details like skin texture without affecting the tones and vice versa. You can smooth out discoloration, wrinkles, or spots on the lower-frequency layer without turning the skin into a blurry mess, preserving that all-important natural texture on the high-frequency layer.

For instance, if you're working on a portrait and the skin looks uneven, you can smooth out the color on the low-frequency layer to create a more uniform skin tone. Meanwhile, all those fine lines, pores, and hair details stay crisp and clear on the high-frequency layer. It's like having your cake and eating it, too: flawless skin that still looks real.

Selective Sharpening to Draw Attention

Now, let's sharpen our focus—literally—with selective sharpening. This isn't about just hitting the 'sharpen' button and calling it a day. Selective sharpening means applying sharpness precisely where you want your viewer's eyes to go. Typically, in a headshot, you want the eyes to be the sharpest part, as they're usually the focal point. But you can also use this technique to bring out details in jewelry, a tie, or even the hair.

The trick is to use a mask. Apply your sharpening to the entire image, then mask areas where you don't want it. This could mean leaving the background slightly softer to make the subject stand out or keeping areas of the skin smoother to avoid emphasizing imperfections. It's like using a spotlight on a stage, directing your audience's attention exactly where you want it.

Composite Techniques for Background Replacement

Lastly, let's dip our toes into the world of composites. Imagine you took a great headshot, but the background could be better. It may be too busy, or it doesn't fit the mood you're going for. With composite techniques, you can place your subject into an entirely different background, making it look like they were there all along. This involves careful selection and masking to separate your subject from the original background and then some finesse in blending them into the new scene. Color matching, shadow casting, and refining edges are all part of the dance to make the composite look seamless.

You can also use compositing to add elements that are not in the original shot. Say you want to add a dramatic flair with some wind-blown hair or perhaps a spectral glow to the frame; composites allow you to layer these elements into your headshot, creating a final image that's more of an art piece than a photograph. It's a playground for creativity, where the only limits are the bounds of your imagination.

As you dive into these advanced techniques, remember that restraint is often as necessary as the technique itself. The best retouching is the kind you don't notice at first glance; it's subtle, enhancing your subject's natural beauty without overshadowing it. So wield these powerful tools with care, and watch your headshots transform into works of art that captivate and charm, one pixel at a time.

The Ethics of Retouching: Maintaining Authenticity

Ah, retouching—the spice of photography! But, like in cooking, too much spice can overpower the dish you're working so hard to perfect. In the context of retouching headshots, it's crucial to find that sweet spot where your edits enhance without deceiving, maintaining the authentic essence of your subject. It's not just about making someone look good; it's about making them look *like themselves* on their best day. Balancing retouching with realism means walking a fine line— removing a temporary blemish is usually fair game, but reshaping facial features? That's where you might want to pump the brakes. The goal is to preserve the integrity of the subject's natural appearance so that when they look at the photo, they see the real person, not an airbrushed illusion.

In this delicate balancing act, communication plays a starring role. It's not just about what *you* think looks best; it's about how the subject sees themselves and wants to be seen. Before you even start editing, chat with your subject about what they expect from the retouching process. Do they want a no-holds-barred glamorous makeover, or are they looking for something subtler? This conversation isn't just a courtesy; it's a crucial step in ensuring that the end product aligns with their vision and comfort level. It's about setting clear expectations and boundaries from the get-go, which helps achieve satisfactory results and builds trust—a currency worth its weight in gold in the photography business.

Now, let's talk about ethical boundaries, to be precise. Every photographer should have them, especially when it comes to retouching. These aren't just about deciding what changes are acceptable; they're about respecting the subject's identity and the trust they place in you as a photographer. For example, consider setting a guideline that any retouching that alters someone's physique or facial structure is off-limits unless specifically requested. These guidelines aren't just to keep you in check; they promise your subjects you'll handle their images with integrity and respect. They ensure that your work remains honest and that the portraits you produce genuinely reflect the person in them, not just your skills with a software tool.

And finally, it's vital to reflect on how retouching can impact the subject's self-image and public perception. In an era where 'Instagram reality' often blurs the lines between natural and dig- itally enhanced, your choices at the editing desk can reinforce or challenge these norms. Overly perfected images can set unrealistic standards and skew perceptions of beauty, leading to social and personal repercussions. As a photographer, you wield more power than you might think— your choices can contribute to a healthier, more realistic portrayal of human beauty, promoting confidence rather than insecurity. By opting for realism and advocating for authenticity, you're not just editing photos; you're helping shape a more honest visual culture, one headshot at a time.

So, as you refine your retouching skills, consider these ethical considerations. They will guide you in creating beautiful, realistic images and building a practice that respects and uplifts your subjects, ensuring that your photography remains as honest as it is impressive. Remember, minor retouching goes a long way, and much integrity goes further.

Color Grading for Mood and Atmosphere

Understanding Color Theory in Post-Processing

Let's talk color, that splash of magic that breathes life into a photograph! Color grading isn't just about tweaking hues; it's about stirring emotions and setting the stage for your headshot to whisper, shout, or serenade. Imagine you're painting with a palette that doesn't just transform the look but also tweaks the feel of your images. This is where a dash of color theory jazzes up our narrative. Every color tugs at our emotions differently—cool blues can soothe the soul, fiery reds might pump up the energy, and earthy greens usually echo calmness. By understanding how colors affect mood, you can use them to enhance or completely transform the atmosphere of your headshots. For instance, a warm, golden tone can give your image a nostalgic, sun-kissed feel, ideal for portraying warmth and approachability. Conversely, a cooler, bluer tone might lend a corporate headshot a sharp, professional edge.

Tools for Color Grading

Now, diving into the tools of the trade, your software is your wand for this magical endeavor. Most post-processing programs offer a delightful array of tools for color grading, with curves and color balance particularly potent. Curves are like the Swiss Army knife of color tools—they let you fine- tune the brightness and contrast and delve deep into adjusting individual color channels. This means you can subtly shift the shadows towards a cooler tone or give the highlights a warm wash, all with a few curve adjustments. Then there's the color balance tool, your go-to for shifting overall color tones without getting lost in the nitty-gritty of curves. It's perfect for adding a quick mood without overcomplicating things. Whether enhancing natural tones or creating something outlandishly artistic, these tools are your best pals.

Creating Style Presets

If you fall in love with a color grading style, why not make it a preset? This is your recipe for that perfect flavor you can apply repeatedly, saving time and ensuring consistency across multiple headshots. Creating presets in your editing software is like meal prepping for the week—you do the hard work upfront, and then it's just smooth sailing. Start by getting your image right with all the color adjustments that tickle your fancy. Then, save these settings as a preset; voila, you've got a one-click wonder for future sessions. This streamlines your workflow and helps you maintain a consistent look, especially when working on a series or a brand portfolio where uniformity is critical.

Examples of Mood Enhancement Through Color

Let's put all this theory into practice with some real-life magic, shall we? Picture a headshot that initially seems a bit flat—good, but not popping. You decide it needs a mood that screams confidence and professionalism. You swing into action, adding a slight blue tint to the shadows for that crisp, clean feel, and you lift the mid-tones into a subtle warmth to keep the skin tones natural and inviting. A before-and-after comparison could show you how much these tweaks shift the vibe—from standard to standout, all through the power of color. Each adjustment changes the visual impact and enhances the emotional response elicited by anyone viewing the headshot.

You transform headshots into compelling narratives by wielding color grading as both a technical skill and a storytelling tool. Each color shift and tonal tweak is a brushstroke in the portrait you are painting of the person behind the lens. Remember, color isn't just seen; it's felt. So, as you play with these hues, think about what you want your audience to feel, and let your colors sing the emotions you wish to convey. This isn't just post-processing; it's mood processing, where you color your canvas's mood and bring your photographic stories to life.

Cropping and Composition Adjustments in Post

Ah, the art of cropping and composition adjustments—think of it as giving your photos a neat little haircut and a dash of good posture. It's where you play the discerning editor, trimming away the unnecessary and tweaking angles to present your subject in the best possible light. Let's dive into how cropping cannot just tidy up your images but also transform them, enhancing the subject's presence and steering clear of distractions that might steal the show from your star performer.

Guidelines for Effective Cropping

Imagine cropping as your secret weapon for turning a good shot into a gallery-worthy masterpiece. It's not just about chopping off edges; it's about reinforcing the story you want the image to tell. Start by asking yourself what the focal point of your headshot is. Is it the eyes? The smile? Or a striking piece of jewelry? Once you've pinpointed your star feature, use cropping to help guide the viewer's eye straight to it. Remove any elements that draw attention away from your focal point. Do you have a stray branch creeping into the frame?

Crop it out. An awkward shadow? Say goodbye. This doesn't just clean up your image; it ensures the viewer's gaze goes precisely where you want it.

But it's not all about cutting things out. The way you crop can also affect how the subject is perceived. Want to convey power and confidence? Crop tightly, allowing the subject to fill the frame, making them seem larger than life. Or, to give a sense of openness and approachability, leave a bit more space around your subject, which can help them appear more relaxed and accessible. These subtle adjustments can significantly shift how the viewer feels about the person they're looking at, turning a simple photo into a compelling narrative.

Aspect Ratio Considerations

Now, let's chat about aspect ratios because, believe it or not, size does matter—at least when it comes to where your photo will be displayed. Whether it's a square frame for Instagram, a wide rectangle for a website banner, or a traditional 8x10 print, each platform has its ideal aspect ratio, and it's your job to ensure your headshot fits perfectly. A mismatch between the photo and its intended space can result in awkward crops — like cutting off the top of someone's head or their chin— which might not be the best look unless you're going for an avant-garde, abstract vibe.

When preparing images for different uses, remember those ratios from the start. Visualize how the image will sit in its digital or physical home. Will text surround it? Does it need to fit within a specific layout? Planning with these questions can save you from making drastic, image-altering crops later, ensuring your headshots always look tailor-made for their space.

Straightening and Perspective Correction

Moving on to straightening and perspective corrections—
it's like ensuring your picture stands up straight, shoulders back, exuding confidence. Even a slight tilt can throw off an image's balance, making it feel unstable or sloppy. Most editing software has easy-to-use straightening tools, so there's no excuse for a slanted horizon or a leaning backdrop. Just a quick slide here or there, and your image is standing tall.

But what about those pesky perspective issues? Your subject may look, or the ba seems unnaturally skewed. Tools like the Lens Correction or Transform functions allow you to adjust the angles and lines, bringing everything back into a more natural and pleasing alignment. It's like having a chiropractic session for your photos, aligning everything to ensure they look their best.

The Art of Recomposition

Finally, let's delve into the subtle art of recomposition through cropping. This isn't just about adjusting what's in your frame; it's about reshaping how the story is told. A slight shift here, a nudge there, and the entire narrative focus of your headshot can shift. For example, cropping closer on a thoughtful expression can turn a simple portrait into an intimate glimpse into the subject's mind. Alternatively, pulling back to include more of the surrounding context can transform a straightforward headshot into a story about the topic and the environment.

This recomposition can be particularly powerful in editorial or commercial photography, where the context can add layers of meaning to the subject's portrayal. It allows you to play with elements like symmetry, leading lines, or the rule of thirds even after the shoot, ensuring that every crop enhances the image's aesthetics and impact. Think of it as having the last word in how your photo is perceived, fine-tuning the final product to ensure it says precisely what you intended.

In headshot photography, cropping and composition adjustments are where precision meets creativity. It's your chance to finish your work, ensuring that every element in the frame serves the story you're trying to tell. So, wield your cropping tool carefully, adjust your angles with an eye for detail, and watch as your headshots transform into precisely composed pieces of personal portrayal, ready to make their mark in the world.

Sharpening and Noise Reduction Strategies

Ah, the dual dance of sharpening and noise reduction in post-processing— it's a bit like adding salt and pepper to your dish. Too little, and it's bland. Too much, and well, you might overpower the whole masterpiece. Let's sprinkle just the right amount to enhance your headshots without losing the essence of what makes them so captivating.

Sharpening Tools and Techniques

Let's talk about sharpening—this is where we make those details pop! But beware, it's easy to fall into the trap of over-sharpening, where your subject's skin might resemble sandpaper rather than human flesh. To steer clear of this, you'll want to get familiar with tools like Unsharp Mask or Smart Sharpen in Photoshop, which offers control over how much and where the sharpening is applied. The trick here is to use a gentle hand. Adjust the sliders for Amount and Radius to subtly enhance the details. Think of it as tuning a guitar; you want to tighten the strings just enough to hit the perfect note, not so much that they snap.

A pro tip? Always zoom in to at least 100% when sharpening. This way, you can see the effects of your adjustments in real time, ensuring you're enhancing details without introducing unwanted artifacts. And remember, the eyes are the windows to the soul, so give them a little extra attention without going overboard. A touch of sharpness can make the eyes clear and striking, drawing the viewer straight into the soul of your subject.

Noise Reduction Without Loss of Detail

Moving onto noise reduction, this is your tool for cleaning up the grain that can creep into your shots, especially those in low light. Noise reduction tools can be found in most editing software, like Lightroom and Capture One, and they work by smoothing out the grain. But here's the kicker—smoothing out can sometimes blur out essential details, turning your sharp shot into a mushy mess. To avoid this, play around with the noise reduction settings, adjusting the luminance and color noise sliders until you find a balance that reduces grain without making the image look like a watercolor painting.

A helpful technique is to apply noise reduction selectively. Use a mask to isolate areas where noise is most problematic, typically the darker or shadow regions, and apply your noise reduction there. This targeted approach allows you to maintain the crispness in areas like the eyes and hair, which are crucial for that sharp, professional look.

Balancing Sharpening and Noise Reduction

Here's where things get crafty—balancing sharpening with noise reduction. It's a delicate operation akin to balancing a seesaw. On one side, you have sharpening that brings out the details; on the other, noise reduction that smooths out imperfections. Lean too much on either side, and your photo loses its equilibrium. Start with light noise reduction to clean up the image. Then, gently apply sharpening to enhance the details. Toggle back and forth between the two until you find that sweet spot where the image looks clean yet detailed.

Continuously monitor the overall image quality as you adjust. It's easy to get lost in the minutiae of sliders and need to remem- ber to step back and look at the bigger picture. Periodically zoom out to view the image as a whole, ensuring that your enhancements improve the photo without detracting from your subject's natural beauty.

Selective Application for Best Results

Lastly, let's champion the cause of selective application. Just like a skilled makeup artist who knows where to contour and where to highlight, you should know where to sharpen and where to smooth. Use layer masks to apply sharpening and noise reduction only to the areas that need them. This method keeps your edits non-destructive and allows for adjustments tailored to each part of the image.

For instance, reduce noise in the background and shadows but keep the sharpness of the facial features and hair. By isolating and treating these areas differently, you ensure that each part of your image receives the attention it needs, resulting in a polished and powerful headshot.

So there you have it—a balanced, selective approach to sharpening and noise reduction that keeps your headshots looking professional, clean, and striking. Remember, the goal is to enhance, not overpower. Keep your edits subtle, and your subjects will shine through naturally, capturing the attention and admiration of all who view them.

Exporting Your Work: Formats and Quality Options

Choosing the Right File Format

Alright, you've edited your heart out, and now it's time to send your headshots into the world. But wait! You can't just hit 'export' and call it a day. Choosing the correct file format is like picking the right outfit for your photo—it needs to match the occasion. JPEG, TIFF, and PNG are like the holy trinity of file formats, each with moments to shine. JPEGs are your go-to for most uses; they're lightweight, universally compatible, and perfect for web use where speed and file size are critical. However, JPEGs use compression that can affect image quality, so they might not be the best choice for printing large-scale or high-quality projects.

Now, when you need all the quality you can get, TIFF is your best friend. It's the file format that only skips on details, storing images without compression so you maintain top-notch quality. Perfect for printing those stunning headshots or storing master files that you might need to revisit and re-edit without losing any data. Then there's PNG, the hero of the web world when transparency is required. Need to place your headshot over a funky background on a website? PNG can handle that gracefully, ensuring your images look crisp without the background boxiness.

Understanding Resolution and Quality Settings

Now, let's talk about resolution and quality because as much as we love high-quality images, nobody wants to download a billboard-sized file when a desktop-sized one will do. Resolution is all about the number of pixels in your image; more pixels mean more detail. But more isn't always better. You need to match the resolution to your intended use. Are you uploading to a web gallery? Stick to around 72 DPI (Dots Per Inch), which looks great on screens and speeds up load times—printing out a portrait to hang above the mantle? You'll want to bump that to at least 300 DPI for sharp, clear prints.

Quality settings are another balancing act. When exporting JPEGs, sliding the quality scale down can reduce file size but push it too far, and your image starts to look like it was taken with a potato. Find a happy medium where the picture looks good and the file size is manageable. This is crucial when sending files to clients or uploading to online galleries where loading speed is vital.

Batch Processing and Exporting

If you're dealing with a batch of headshots from a corporate event or a large family reunion, batch processing is your savior. Most photo editing software allows you to simultaneously apply the same settings to multiple photos. This means you can adjust all your images for web use, apply the same color grading, or resize them in one fell swoop. It saves time and ensures consistency across your collection, which is essential for maintaining a professional look.

Setting up batch processing usually involves a few clicks in your software's export dialogue. You select the standard settings, choose where to save the files, and let the computer do its thing while you grab a well-deserved coffee. By the time you're back, all your photos are ready to go, each tweaked to perfection and uniform in style and format.

Protecting Your Work with Watermarks

Last but not least, let's talk about protecting your work. Watermarks are like your personal stamp, a way to safeguard your images from being used without your permission or at least without giving you credit. But here's the kicker: they need to be subtle. A giant watermark across the middle of your image might protect it, but it also distracts from the photograph's beauty. Instead, aim for something small and discreet, placed in the corner or along the edge. It should be visible enough to be noticed if someone is looking but not so bold as to interfere with the image itself.

Creating a watermark usually involves logo design and more fun with your editing software. Create a simple text watermark or design a small logo if you're feeling fancy. Then, it's just a matter of adding it to your images in a non-destructive layer before you export them. This way, you keep your brand visible without compromising the integrity of your photographs.

So, as you prepare to send your headshots off into the world, think of these steps as the final checks and balances. Choosing the correct format and settings, using batch processing to keep things consistent, and subtly marking your work with a watermark are all crucial steps to ensure your images make their mark for all the right reasons. With these tools in your belt, you're ready to confidently share your work, knowing it's presented at its best and protected against misuse. Now, go forth and export!

Creating a Cohesive Look for Your Portfolio

The Importance of Consistency

Think of your portfolio as your photography playlist—it should sing in harmony, making your style unmistakable at first glance. Consistency isn't just about making things match; it's about setting a signature vibe that threads through your work like a catchy chorus in a hit song. This goes beyond just shooting with the same camera or lens; it's about how each image reflects a consistent quality, tone, and mood that says 'you' all over them. Whether it's the lighting style, the posing, or the post- processing flair, each element should contribute to a cohesive whole. Why? When your portfolio feels like a well-orchestrated symphony rather than a random mixtape, it appeals more to clients and elevates your brand, making you and your work more recognizable and more in demand.

Using Presets and Actions

Let's jazz things up with some time-saving magic—presets and actions. These are like your personal shortcuts in the editing process, ensuring each photo isn't just edited but carries your unique stamp of consistency. Creating presets in your editing software is like setting up a custom filter that applies your favorite adjustments with one click. Whether it's a specific contrast level, a color overlay, or a particular curve setting, presets allow you to maintain a uniform look effortlessly across various shoots.

But why stop at presets? Dive into the world of actions. Actions in Photoshop, for instance, are like recording your favorite song so you can play it back anytime. They record your editing steps and allow you to replay them on different images. This can be incredibly handy for repetitive tasks like resizing, sharpening, or applying specific adjustments. Using these tools ensures that every image meets your high standards and strengthens your portfolio's visual identity.

Portfolio Selection and Curation

Selecting and curating the right images for your portfolio is akin to crafting a gourmet menu—it should whet the appetite and leave them wanting more. Start by choosing images that showcase your range but also highlight your strengths. Have an epic headshot that stops viewers in their tracks? Make it a centerpiece. A series that tells a compelling story? Include it to show your narrative skills. But here's the key: diversity within unity. Your chosen images should be varied enough to show your versatility but similar style and quality to reinforce your brand's identity.

Curation is not just about selection; it's about arrangement. Organize your images to complement each other, leading viewers on a journey that progressively showcases your skills and style. Think of it as arranging the tracks in an album— they should flow into one another, creating an engaging and cohesive experience.

Evolving Your Style Without Losing Cohesion

Let's face it: staying static in a dynamic field like photography can feel like playing yesterday's hits—familiar but possibly outdated. Evolving your style is crucial, but how do you do it without losing the cohesive look of your portfolio? The trick lies in gradual, thoughtful changes that are more like remixes than complete genre switches. Start by integrating new techniques or trends into your work incrementally. Test these innovations in a few projects and see how they enhance your style.

As you evolve, update your portfolio regularly to reflect these changes. Replace older images with new ones that showcase your latest skills and artistic growth. However, ensure these new additions harmonize with the existing work regarding quality and overall vibe. This way, your portfolio remains fresh yet familiar, continuously attracting clients with your evolving, consistent, artistic narrative.

In essence, crafting a cohesive portfolio is about finding the perfect balance between variety and uniformity. It's about ensuring every image sings harmoniously with your unique style, making your work instantly recognizable. As you curate this visual symphony, remember that each photo is a note in the melody of your career, and how you compose them can turn your portfolio from a mere collection of images into a compelling showcase of your photographic journey.

Wrapping Up: From Shooting to Showcasing

As we close this chapter on creating a cohesive look for your portfolio, remember that the journey from capturing to showcasing is a continuous loop of learning, developing, and refining. Whether mastering the nuances of post-processing or curating a portfolio that resonates with your artistic voice, each step is crucial in crafting a body of work reflecting your skills and unique perspective as an artist. Keep pushing your creativity's boundaries, refining your techniques, and, most importantly, staying true to your style. Next, we dive deeper into the business side of things, where we'll translate your artistic efforts into commercial success. So, stay tuned, keep your lenses clean and your minds open as we continue to explore the vast, exciting world of photography.

Chapter 5: Business, Marketing, and Building Your Brand

Imagine this: you've just nailed that perfect headshot session. The lighting was spot on, your subject was grinning ear to ear, and the images are so good that you're already dreaming of the rave reviews. But wait, before you dive into the world of likes, shares, and glowing comments, let's channel some of that creative gusto into setting up the nuts and bolts of your headshot photography business. After all, even the most artistic of us can't shy away from the nitty-gritty of business fundamentals if we want to turn our passion into our paycheck!

Setting Up Your Headshot Photography Business

Business Registration and Legalities

First things first, let's talk legality. Registering your business might sound as dry as day-old toast, but it's essential. You wouldn't drive a car without registering it. The same goes for your business. This process gives your venture legitimacy and protects your assets from business liabilities. Depending on where you reside, you'll start by registering your business name—something catchy that sticks in people's minds—and then move on to obtaining the necessary permits and licenses. It's like getting a passport for your business, allowing you to operate without bumping into legal hurdles. Check with your local city hall or a business advisor for specifics. Each area has its own set of rules, and you want to make sure you're as compliant as a cat following the scent of tuna.

Choosing a Business Structure

Next up is picking a business structure, and oh boy, does this matter! Are you a lone wolf? Consider a Sole Proprietorship. If you're all about that 'sharing is caring' vibe and having a partner, then a Partnership might be your jam. Feeling fancy and want that sweet, sweet liability protection? An LLC (Limited Liability Company) could be your best bet. Each structure affects your taxes, liability, and even your role within your company, so choose wisely. It's like picking a character in a video game; each has strengths and weaknesses!

Setting Up a Home Studio vs. Renting Space

Now, where to set up shop? Transforming a part of your home into a studio is budget-friendly and incredibly convenient. Imagine rolling out of bed, grabbing a coffee, and stepping into your studio—slippers. However, space and professionalism can be limiting. On the flip side, renting a space screams professionalism and keeps home and work separate, but it's a significant overhead, and hey, you'll have to put on real pants. Weigh these options based on your business goals, budget, and personal work style.

Essential Gear and Software Investments

Let's talk gear and software, the bread and butter of your business. Start with the essentials: a good camera, prime lenses (oh, that beautiful bokeh!), and some essential lighting equipment. Remember editing software like Adobe Photoshop or Lightroom; these are your digital darkrooms. Now, while it's tempting to splurge on the fanciest gear, remember, the wizard, not the wand, makes the magic happen. Start with what you need to produce quality work, and upgrade as your business grows. A world of budget-friendly options won't break the bank but will still get you those head-turning shots.

So there you have it, the scaffolding around which you can build your headshot photography empire (or cozy cottage if that's more your vibe) from the legality dance to the cozy-vs.-cosmopolitan studio debate, each decision crafts the backbone of a uniquely your business. Remember, the goal here isn't just to create art; it's to create a sustainable business that allows you to pursue your passion for photography daily. So take these first steps seriously, but don't forget to have a little fun along the way—after all, it's not just a business; it's your passion turned into a profession!

Pricing Strategies for Your Services

Understanding Your Market

So, you've got your camera ready, your studio set up just right, and your skills are sharper than a tack—what's next? Ah, the ever-intimidating task of setting your prices. Before you pull numbers out of thin air, let's get down to some serious business reconnaissance. Understanding your local market is like being a detective in your backyard. You're not just spying on the competition to see who's charging what but understanding why they're charging those rates. It's all about context. Are they offering quick 30-minute sessions or a full-day affair with makeup and wardrobe changes? Dive into their service lists, peek at their portfolios, and if you're feeling particularly bold, why not book a session? Experience their service and see what your future clients might expect from you.

This sleuthing gives you a benchmark. But remember, it's not just about matching or undercutting prices. It's about understanding the value behind those numbers. What are clients in your area willing to pay? This might involve some trial and error coupled with feedback gathering. Surveys, informal chats post-session, and keeping an eye on how quickly (or slowly) your bookings fill up can provide invaluable insights into your market's price sensitivity. It's about finding that sweet spot where your price meets your clients' perception of your value.

Creating Pricing Packages

Now, with your detective hat still on, let's talk packages. Creating pricing packages isn't just slapping together a few services and calling it a day—it's about crafting experiences your clients can choose from, much like a menu at a fancy restaurant. Each package should cater to different needs and budgets. Start with a basic package, something that covers your essentials. Then, build up to more premium options, including additional features like extra time, more photos, special editing, or even wardrobe changes. This tiered approach caters to a broader range of clients and gently nudges customers towards higher-value options.

When constructing these packages, keep clarity in mind. Each package should clearly state what it includes, how much it costs, and what makes it different. This clarity helps clients feel informed and confident in their choices, reducing the back-and-forth that can often delay bookings. Plus, who doesn't appreciate knowing exactly what they're getting into? It's like seeing the ingredients listed on your smoothie; it feels right.

Communicating Value to Clients

Speaking of feeling right, let's talk about communicating the value of your services. This is where your inner salesperson needs to shine, not by being pushy but by being transparent and passionate about your offer. Start by highlighting what sets your headshots apart. Do you provide an unrivaled turnaround time? Are your lighting techniques straight out of a fairy tale? It could be your ability to make clients feel at ease, a not-so-minor feat in the often nerve-wracking experience of being in front of a camera. Whatever your strengths, ensure they're front and center in your conversations, website, and marketing materials.

But it's not just about what you say; it's about how you make your clients feel. Ensure that every interaction, from the initial inquiry to the final delivery, is smooth, professional, and personalized. When clients understand the effort, skill, and care that goes into creating their headshots, they're more likely to appreciate the value and less likely to quibble over price. It's about building that trust and appreciation that turns first-time clients into lifelong fans.

Adjusting Prices as Your Business Grows

Lastly, let's not forget that your pricing isn't set in stone. As your skills sharpen, your portfolio expands, and your reputation soars, your prices should reflect that growth. Reviewing your prices periodically—say, annually—allows you to adjust them to better reflect your current standing in the market. Maybe you've invested in better gear, attended a prestigious workshop, or honed your craft to near perfection. All these developments can justify a price adjustment that your clients, especially the repeat ones, will likely understand and respect.

Raising prices can be nerve-wracking, but it can be a seamless transition if done thoughtfully. Communicate changes ahead of time and explain the reasons behind the increase. Offer grandfathering rates to existing clients or a booking window at old prices before the new ones take effect. This approach not only eases your clients into the transition but also shows that you value their loyalty, making the pill of price increase a tad sweeter to swallow.

So, there you go; from understanding your market to adjusting your prices, these strategies are about much more than just numbers. They are about building a sustainable business that respects your worth as a photographer and meets your client's needs with professionalism and care. Remember, every price tag you set reflects your confidence in your craft, so wear it proudly.

Marketing 101 for Headshot Photographers

Identifying Your Ideal Client

Let's start by playing a little matchmaker between you and your future clients. Identifying your ideal client isn't about setting up a profile on a dating app, but it's pretty close! Think about who would most appreciate and require your services. Are you aiming to capture the corporate climbers needing a sleek, professional look for LinkedIn? Or are you more into the creative crowd, where artists and musicians seek something that screams originality? You may be passionate about helping everyday folks see their best selves through a lens. Whoever it is, sketching out a clear profile of these individuals helps tailor your marketing strategies directly to those who will happily open their wallets for your skills.

Start by considering demographics like age, occupation, and lifestyle. For instance, young professionals might prefer a quick, efficient session with digital-only packages, while actors might need multiple outfit changes and physical prints for casting calls. Understanding these nuances allows you to craft marketing messages that resonate deeply, making potential clients feel like you're speaking directly to them. And let's be honest, who doesn't like feeling a bit special?

Developing a Marketing Plan

With your ideal client in mind, it's time to whip up a marketing plan as detailed as your camera settings. This plan is your roadmap, guiding you on online and offline client engagement paths. Start with a robust online strategy—this is your website, social media, and email marketing. Your website should be as polished as your best headshot, showcasing your portfolio and making it easy for clients to book sessions. Social media platforms like Instagram and Pinterest are your galleries, where your work does the talking and walking, attracting clients with each post.

Remember the power of email marketing. A well-crafted newsletter can keep you at the top of clients' minds, sharing updates, promotions, and tips that keep them engaged. For offline strategies, think local. Participate in community events or photography fairs. We could even host a workshop. These face-to-face interactions build trust and familiarity, turning locals into loyal clients. And remember, every flyer, business card, or poster you hand out should reflect the quality and style of your photography. Consistency is critical to creating a brand identity that sticks.

Leveraging Word-of-Mouth

Word-of-mouth is the old-school social network that can make or break businesses. In photography, a glowing recommendation from a satisfied client is worth its weight in gold. Encourage this goldmine by making each client interaction stellar. From the moment they book to the moment they receive their final images, ensure they feel valued and satisfied. Happy clients are chatty clients—they'll sing your praises to friends, family, and even that stranger in the coffee line.

To give them a little nudge, why not introduce a referral program? Offer a discount or a freebie for every new client they bring to you. It's a win-win; they get a deal, and you get a new client. Make sharing their great experience easy, too. Please provide them with shareable digital images or branded hashtags they can use when posting their photos online. Every tagged post is a free advertisement, directly reaching your target audience.

Measuring Marketing Success

Finally, to ensure your marketing isn't just a shot in the dark, you must measure its effectiveness. This is where analytics come into play. Dive into the data from your website and social media platforms. Tools like Google Analytics and Instagram Insights can show you who's visiting your pages, how long they stay, and what content they interact with the most. Are visitors clicking on the 'Book Now' button? Which posts are getting the most likes or shares? This information is a goldmine for understanding what's working and what's not.

Set clear goals for your marketing efforts, whether increasing website traffic, boosting session bookings, or growing your social media following. Then, regularly review your progress towards these goals. Feel free to tweak your strategies if you need to hit your marks. Marketing is an ongoing experiment; what doesn't work today might be tomorrow's breakthrough with some adjustments.

By closely monitoring these metrics, you will become more adept at reaching your ideal clients and continuously improving your marketing game. It's like fine-tuning your camera settings—adjust, shoot, and repeat until everything clicks perfectly. With each adjustment, your marketing strategies will become more effective, driving more clients to your door, ready to strike a pose.

Social Media and Online Presence: Building Your Brand

Choosing the Right Platforms

Navigating the bustling social media landscape is like attending a massive party and deciding who to chat with. You can only mingle with some, so you choose based on interests, vibes, and where you will most likely make meaningful connections! In the realm of photography, not all platforms are created equal when it comes to showcasing your headshot prowess. With its visual-centric layout, Instagram is the belle of the ball for photographers. It's where your stunning headshots can truly pop and attract immediate attention.

Pinterest, too, serves as a fantastic gallery for your work, appealing particularly to those planning events or looking to update their professional portfolios.

Then there's LinkedIn, the professional networking giant. It's not just for suits and corporate speak; it's also a goldmine for photographers specializing in professional headshots. Here, you can connect directly with professionals who value and require high-quality personal branding images. The trick is to choose platforms where your target clients are already hanging out and engaging. Each platform has its language and etiquette, so once you pick your party spot, speak the lingo. Share content that resonates with the specific audience of that platform—whether it's behind-the-scenes shots on Instagram, pin-worthy editorial headshots on Pinterest, or before-and-after transformations on LinkedIn.

Creating Engaging Content

Now, about making waves with your content—think of each post as a mini-story where your headshots are the protagonists. The plot? Showing off your skill and versatility. Instagram loves a good narrative, so why not share the story behind am particular shoot? Talk about the challenges, the on-the-spot creative decisions, or how you brought a client's vision to life. These stories showcase your technical skills and humanize your brand, making potential clients feel connected and confident in your hands.

But let's not stop at images. Videos are like the secret sauce of social media engagement. A quick time-lapse of your editing process or a heartfelt testimonial from a satisfied client can boost your content's engagement. Also, consider live sessions or Q&As where you interact directly with your followers, answering their burning questions or giving live critiques or tutorials. This interactive content spikes engagement and builds trust and authority in your niche.

Building a Professional Website

Your website is your digital storefront, and just like any high-street shop, its layout, signage, and the goodies inside determine whether people walk in or stroll by. To convert visitors into clients, ensure your website mirrors your professionalism and artistic flair. Start with a clean, easy-to-navigate layout. No one enjoys a treasure hunt when they're just trying to view your portfolio or book a session. Speaking of portfolios, yours should be front and center—beautifully displayed with high-resolution images that load faster than you can say 'cheese.'

Include an 'About Me' section where your personality shines. People don't just buy services; they buy relationships. Let them know who you are, why you love what you do, and what makes your approach unique. And, of course, don't hide your contact information in a corner. Make it prominent with a simple, straightforward booking process. An online booking system? Even better. It's like offering your clients a VIP pass to your schedule, letting them choose their spot without back-and- forth emails.

SEO Basics for Photographers

Let's demystify SEO (Search Engine Optimization) because what good is a stunning website if no one can find it? Think of SEO as the beacon that guides clients through the vast ocean of the internet straight to your shores. Start with keyword research. Tools like Google Keyword Planner or Moz Keyword Explorer can help you understand what potential clients are searching for. Are they looking for 'professional headshot photographers,' 'corporate headshots,' or 'actor headshots'? Once you know, sprinkle these keywords across your website— your titles, descriptions, and content.

But SEO isn't just about keywords. Google loves quality and relevance. Ensure your website is updated regularly with fresh content that answers your clients' questions. Start a blog where you share tips on preparing for a headshot session or the latest trends in professional photography. Also, optimize your website's mobile version. More people than ever are browsing on their phones, and a mobile-friendly site boosts your SEO ranking significantly.

Engaging in these strategies transforms your online presence from passive to dynamic, turning your digital spaces into active tools that work tirelessly to attract and convert clients. From choosing the right platforms to optimizing your website for search engines, every step enhances your visibility and allure in the digital world. Keep your content fresh and your interactions genuine, and watch as your online presence becomes just as powerful and persuasive as your photography.

Client Consultations: Winning Strategies and Common Pitfalls

Imagine stepping into a meeting where you're presenting your portfolio and pitching your persona, your process, and the essence of your brand. That's what client consultations are all about. They're not merely appointments but golden opportunities to convert inquiries into booked sessions. But, as with all golden opportunities, they come with their own set of challenges and triumphs. So, let's unpack some strategies to ensure your consultations are less 'oops' and more 'oooh.'

Preparing for Consultations

Stepping into a consultation unprepared is like going on stage without knowing your lines—it can be a disaster waiting to happen. Preparation is critical, and it starts with understanding precisely what you need to cover during these meetings. Begin by outlining the flow of the consultation. Think of it as scripting a play where every act matters. Start with a warm introduction where you introduce yourself and set a welcoming tone for the meeting. Transition smoothly into discussing your portfolio. Here's a pro tip: don't just show your best shots; choose the ones that best align with the client's needs, which you've already sniffed out from their initial inquiry.

Next up, dive into the specifics of your services. What packages do you offer? Are there customization options? What's the turnaround time? Be clear and concise, giving them just enough information to grasp the value of what you're offering without overwhelming them. And don't forget to discuss the logistics— location, timing, and what they need to bring or prepare. Ending this phase with a clear call to action, like choosing a package or scheduling a session, keeps the ball rolling.

Building Rapport

While it's excellent to technically have all your ducks in a row, building a rapport with potential clients seals the deal. Rapport is the bridge that connects your professional prowess to their personal needs. Start by actively listening. Yes, you have your script but be flexible. Let them express their visions, concerns, and expectations. This isn't just polite—it's strategic. It helps tailor your pitch to align with their specific needs, making your service feel bespoke, even if it's a package deal.

Engage with their stories. If they mention their upcoming job interview, chat about how the right headshot can make a memorable first impression. This personal touch makes clients feel valued and subtly stitches your services into the fabric of their needs. It's about making the consultation a conversation rather than a sales pitch. Remember, people are more likely to book services when they feel connected, not just when they're impressed by their skills.

Handling Objections

No matter how slick your presentation or how charming your chatter is, objections are as common as clouds on a rainy day. Maybe it's the price, the package details, or the timing—

whatever the concern, handle it with grace and professionalism. First, understand that objections are not rejections. They're opportunities for clarification, reassurance, and sometimes, negotiation.

For instance, when a client balks at the price, don't just slash your rates to make the sale. Instead, revisit the value of what you're offering. Break it down—highlight the expertise, personalized attention, and high-quality outcomes. If the objection concerns the scope of services, clarify or suggest alternatives that better suit their needs and budget. Always keep the door open for future negotiations by suggesting tailored solutions that could work within their parameters.

Follow-up After Consultations

The curtain may close on the consultation, but the show is far from over. Many photographers drop the ball on follow-up. Don't be that person. Whether it's a simple thank-you email, a summary of what was discussed, or answers to questions during the meeting, timely follow-ups keep you and your services in the client's mind.

But here's the real kicker: timing your follow-up can dramatically boost your booking rates. Strike while the iron is hot, typically within 24 to 48 hours post-consultation. This not only shows professionalism but also eagerness and dedication to client satisfaction. Include a direct call-to-action in your follow-up—maybe a link to finalize the booking or a reminder of the discussed schedule. Make it as easy as possible for them to say yes.

Mastering client consultations is an art form that combines preparation, personal connection, and persistence. It's about making potential clients feel heard, valued, and excited about possibly working with you. So, as you refine your consultation strategies, remember that each meeting is a stage, and you're the star. Shine brightly, connect genuinely, and watch those consultation slots turn into booked and busy photography sessions.

Managing Client Expectations and Deliverables

Setting Clear Expectations

Imagine setting out on a road trip without a map or GPS. Without a clear route, unexpected detours could occur, and reaching your destination would likely take longer. Well, managing client expectations is quite similar to planning a smooth journey. From the very first interaction, it's crucial to lay out a roadmap of what your clients can expect during their headshot session. This means discussing everything from the shoot's deliverables to the expected timelines and even the nitty-gritty of post-processing. Clarity at this stage helps preempt misunderstandings and sets a tone of professionalism.

Start by creating a client welcome pack or a detailed guide that outlines each step of your process. Include what they must bring, how they should prepare, and what happens after the shoot. For instance, explain how many images they will receive, how they will select their favorites, and how long the editing process will typically take. This guide makes your clients feel well-informed and reassures them that they are in capable hands. Remember, informed clients are happy clients —they know what to expect and are much more likely to be satisfied with the outcome.

Effective Communication Throughout the Project

Keeping the lines of communication open throughout the project is like keeping the radio tuned to the right station during that road trip. It ensures everyone sings along to the same tune and enjoys the ride. Regular updates can do wonders for maintaining a good rapport with clients. Whether it's a quick email to confirm a session date, a message to let them know their proofs are ready for viewing, or a check-in during the editing process to gather feedback, these little touches make the client feel valued and involved.

Consider setting up scheduled check-ins at various project stages, especially for larger or more involved shoots. This could be through emails, phone calls, or even a personalized client portal on your website where they can see the status of their project. Tools like these keep your clients informed and save you from the avalanche of 'just checking in' emails that can pile up and consume your time. Effective communication makes the process as transparent and seamless as possible, removing potential stress points.

Delivering on Promises

Now, delivering on promises is where you get to shine. It's

one thing to talk about a good game, but play it? That's where the magic happens. Meeting your deadlines, providing high-quality images, and adhering to the specifics of your client agreement all fall under this umbrella. If you promised a two-week turnaround, do all you can to stick to that timeline. If you agree to provide 20 edited images, ensure you meet (or exceed) that number. Consistently delivering on your promises builds trust and reliability, two pillars that can elevate your reputation from good to stellar.

But why stop at just meeting expectations when you can exceed them? Throw in a few extra edits, delivered earlier than anticipated, or add a small thank-you note or gift when returning the final images. Small gestures like these can turn a satisfied client into a lifelong advocate for your business. They're the unexpected playlist that turns a good road trip into an unforgettable adventure.

Handling Dissatisfied Clients

Despite your best efforts, there will be times when clients aren't thrilled with the outcome. They may have envisioned something different, or there needed to be better communication. Handling dissatisfied clients gracefully is crucial; consider it a test of your customer service skills. First, listen actively. Give them space to express their concerns without interruption. Often, just feeling heard can diffuse frustration and open the door to finding a solution.

Once you understand their concerns, evaluate what can be done to rectify the situation. Can the images be re-edited? Is a reshoot a feasible option? Offer practical solutions where possible. If the dissatisfaction stems from unmet expectations that were unclear from the start, consider this a learning moment to refine how you communicate your services and manage expectations in the future.

Maintaining professionalism is critical in cases where a resolution could be more straightforward. Explain calmly what can and cannot be done, always emphasizing your desire to ensure their satisfaction within the bounds of your established policies. Turning a negative experience into a positive one can sometimes transform a disgruntled client into your most vocal supporter, proving that challenges, when handled well, are opportunities in disguise.

Navigating client relationships through clear expectations, open communication, and a commitment to delivering quality is more than just good business practice; it's an art form that builds your brand's reputation, one satisfied client at a time. So, keep steering that wheel with confidence and care, knowing every interaction is a step toward building a resilient, respected photography business.

Navigating the Challenges of Freelance Photography

Time Management

Ah, time management—the mythical beast every freelancer tries to tame! When juggling photoshoots, editing, marketing, and the never-ending administrative tasks, it can feel like you're spinning plates while riding a unicycle. But fear not; with a few clever strategies, you can keep those plates spinning without a sweat. Start by embracing the power of scheduling. Think of your daily schedule as a recipe; each ingredient needs cooking time. Allocate specific blocks of time for shooting, editing, answering emails, and even scrolling through social media (we all do it; let's be confirmed). Tools like Google Calendar or Trello can be lifesavers, helping you visualize your week at a glance and adjust on the fly.

Another hot tip? Prioritize like a pro. Not all tasks are created equal. Identify your most critical actions—directly affecting your income or client satisfaction—and tackle them first. Everything else can wait. Also, don't forget to set aside time for unexpected tasks or delays. Let's face it: no day goes perfectly to plan, especially in the dynamic world of photography. A buffer period can keep you from feeling flustered when things inevitably go sideways.

Lastly, consider batching similar tasks together. Power through all your editing in one go, or set a day just for client consultations. This approach minimizes the constant mental gear-shifting that can wear you down and consume your time. By streamlining your tasks, you work more efficiently and free up chunks of time to relax or pursue personal projects, keeping the creative juices flowing without burnout.

Maintaining Work-Life Balance

Speaking of burnout, maintaining a healthy work-life balance is not just an excellent idea—it's essential for your sanity and creativity. When your home is your office, it's tempting to blur the lines between personal and work time. Who hasn't thought, "I'll just do a bit of editing before bed," only to find themselves at the computer at midnight? To avoid this, set clear boundaries, have a designated workspace, stick to defined working hours, and when the workday is done, close the door —or at least shut down the computer—and step back into your personal life.

Make sure to schedule downtime like you would a client meeting. It's that important. Engage in activities that recharge your batteries. Regular breaks prevent burnout and enhance your creativity, whether it's yoga, a movie night, or a peaceful walk. Remember, a well-rested photographer is a more productive and creative photographer.

Also, try to automate or outsource tasks that suck up your time without providing much value. Whether it's accounting, social media management, or even housekeeping, freeing up more time to focus on what you love and excel at can vastly improve your quality of life and job satisfaction. This investment in your well-being pays dividends in terms of productivity and happiness.

Dealing with Inconsistent Income

Now, onto one of the scariest parts of freelancing—the feast-or-famine nature of income. One month, you're the king of the world, booking back-to-back shoots; the next, you wonder if your email is broken because it's so quiet. First, it's crucial to budget wisely. During those feast periods, resist the urge to splurge. Save some of your income for leaner months, and consider diversifying your revenue streams. Maybe sell prints online, offer workshops, or venture into stock photography. Having multiple income sources can buffer against slow periods and reduce financial stress.

Another savvy move is to build an emergency fund. Aim for three to six months' worth of expenses saved up. This safety net can be a lifesaver when clients are sparse. It also gives you the freedom to be selective about the projects you take on, ensuring you can always work on jobs that truly resonate with your artistic vision.

Finding Support and Resources

Last but not least, let's talk about the power of community. Freelancing can be isolating, but remember, you're not alone. Connecting with other photographers through online forums, social media groups, or local meet-ups can be incredibly enriching. These connections can lead to friendships, collaborations, and learning opportunities from others' experiences. Plus, sharing your struggles and successes with people who understand what you're going through is always comforting.

Remember to never underestimate the value of mentorship, too. Finding a mentor who has navigated the freelance maze can provide guidance, inspiration, and practical tips tailored to your specific challenges. In return, consider mentoring someone else. Teaching can be a fantastic way to solidify your knowledge and give back to the community supporting you.

Participating in photography groups and attending workshops helps you stay up-to-date with industry trends and keeps you connected to the creative pulse of your profession. The inspiration and energy from these interactions fuel your passion and drive for photography, making the freelance journey less daunting and much more rewarding.

So, as you navigate the wild waters of freelance photography, remember these strategies: Manage your time wisely, keep your work and personal life balanced, plan for financial ups and downs, and immerse yourself in the supportive community of fellow photographers. With these practices in place, you'll survive and thrive in the freelance lifestyle.

Legal and Ethical Considerations in Professional Photography

Navigating professional photography's legal and ethical land-scape isn't just about keeping your gear in line; it's about ensuring your entire operation is on the straight and narrow. Think of it as the rule book that keeps the game fair and fun for everyone involved. Now, let's crack open this rule book, starting with the basics of copyright law. You know that feeling of pride when you snap that perfect shot? Well, when your camera clicks, you automatically hold the copyright to that image. This means you are the sole person who can decide how your photos are used, whether printed, posted online, or sold. But here's the kicker—it's all about having proof. So, consider registering your photographs with the copyright office. It's like putting a giant "mine" label on your work, which can be handy should someone decide your art looks better on their website without your permission.

Now, onto contracts and model releases. If copyright law locks your studio door, consider contracts and model releases for the security cameras. They protect you and your clients by clearly laying out expectations, deliverables, and permissions. For every shoot, have a contract that details everything from payment terms to how the images can be used. Model releases are incredibly crucial. They ensure your models have consented to their images to be used commercially, covering you against privacy claims. It's like asking permission before posting that hilarious photo of your friend asleep with pizza on their face. It ensures everyone's happy and on the same page.

But let's remember the ethical side of things. Photography, especially headshots, is intensely personal. Respecting client privacy and accurately representing your subjects is paramount. This means being honest about what you can deliver and ensuring your client's data and images are handled carefully. If you're editing, keep it accurate—no changing their appearance so much that their mother wouldn't recognize them. It's about enhancing, not altering, reality. And when it comes to sharing client images in your portfolio or on social media, always get permission. Just think how you'd feel if someone shared your photo without asking—probably a bit miffed, right? It's about treating your clients with the respect and professionalism they deserve.

Lastly, staying informed about legal changes is crucial. Laws and regulations around digital content, privacy, and copyright are as dynamic as the technology driving them. Keeping up-to-date is more than just good practice; protecting yourself and your business is essential. Subscribe to photography and legal newsletters, join professional groups, or even set up Google alerts for terms like "photography copyright law changes." Think of this as your radar system, helping you navigate and adapt to the ever-changing legal landscape of the photography world.

By wrapping your head around these legal and ethical considerations, you safeguard your business and build trust with your clients. It shows that you're not just about taking great photos—you're about doing it the right way, respecting both the art and the legalities that come with it. This commitment to integrity sets you apart in the crowded world of photography, making you not just a skilled photographer but a reputable one. So, keep your legal ducks in a row and your ethical compass set straight, and you'll not only avoid potential legal headaches but also build a respected business for its professionalism and integrity.

Building and Presenting a Compelling Portfolio

Imagine your portfolio as your gallery, a curated collection showcasing your technical skills and telling your artistic journey's story. It's your chance to make a stellar first impression, so let's make sure it's like that unforgettable opening scene of a blockbuster movie. When selecting the best work for your portfolio, think of it as choosing the leading stars for a film. These images should be technically free and demonstrate your range and adaptability. Include a variety of headshots that show different expressions, lighting techniques, and backgrounds. This variety helps potential clients see your versatility and imagine themselves through your lens. Remember, each photo should have a reason for being in your portfolio. One may show off your knack for dramatic lighting, while another captures a raw, emotional expression that tells a story without words. It's about quality over quantity; choose wisely to keep your audience engaged and wanting more.

Tailoring your portfolio to your target market is like customizing a pitch to fit a specific audience—it increases your chance of hitting the bullseye. Start by understanding who your ideal clients are. Do the actors need dynamic headshots for casting? Or professionals looking for sleek, business-like portraits for LinkedIn? Once you have a clear picture, you can tailor your portfolio to resonate with them. This might mean highlighting corporate headshots and clean, straightforward compositions for business professionals or showcasing more creative, expressive shots for artists and performers. Consider creating separate sections or even different portfolios for each market segment. This targeted approach shows potential clients that you understand their specific needs and are skilled at fulfilling them.

In the digital age, how you present your portfolio can be just as important as what's in it. Online portfolios offer the convenience and accessibility that today's clients expect. They allow your work to be just a click away from potential clients worldwide. Ensure your online portfolio is easy to navigate, loads quickly, and displays beautifully on all devices. High-quality images and a sleek, professional design reflect the caliber of your work. However, take into account the power of a physical portfolio. There's something undeniably impactful about holding a beautifully printed photograph. It engages the sense of touch and adds a layer of luxury and seriousness to your presentation. Physical portfolios can be particularly effective in face-to-face meetings, where the tactile quality of the prints can make a strong, memorable statement. The key is to use both online and physical portfolios to your advantage, ensuring they complement each other and cater to different viewing preferences.

Keeping your portfolio updated is crucial in maintaining its relevance and appeal. As your skills grow and your style evolves, so should your portfolio. Regularly revisiting and revising your collection ensures it accurately reflects your current abilities and artistic direction. This might mean saying goodbye to older works that no longer represent your best or are out of sync with your current style. It also means adding fresh content that showcases new techniques you've mastered or new experiences you've gained. An updated portfolio demonstrates your development and commitment to your craft and keeps your presentation fresh and exciting for repeat visitors. It shows that you are active, evolving, and continuously pushing the boundaries of your art.

As you build and refine your portfolio, remember it's more than just a collection of images. It reflects your unique vision and skills, is a tool to connect with potential clients, and is a bridge to new opportunities. So invest the time and thought it deserves, and watch as it opens doors to new possibilities and paths in your photography career.

Expanding Your Network: Collaborations and Community Engagement

Let's discuss spreading your creative wings and diving into the big, beautiful world of networking and collaboration. Now, I know what you might think—networking sounds as fun as organizing your tax receipts. But trust me, with a pinch of strategy and a dash of your natural charm; it can be as rewarding as nailing that perfect shot on a tricky lighting day. So, why network? Well, rubbing elbows with fellow photographers and other creatives isn't just about swapping business cards and following each other on Instagram. It's about building a community that supports, inspires, and drives everyone forward. Imagine creating your creative eco-system, where everyone brings something unique.

Engaging with other photographers, especially those who might share your niche, can open up a treasure trove of opportunities. From co-hosting workshops that showcase your collective skills to sharing gigs when your plate is overflowing, the benefits are as plentiful as SD cards at a wedding shoot. But here's the real kicker—referrals. Yes, in an industry where trust is king, having a network of peers who trust your work enough to recommend you to their clients can be golden. It's like having a team of unofficial marketing agents, all because you took the time to build genuine connections.

And speaking of connections, let's pay attention to the magic of collaborating with makeup artists and stylists. These artists are not just about making people look good; they're about transforming your headshots into works of art. Imagine this: you're set to shoot a corporate headshot. Pretty standard stuff, right? But add a stylist into the mix, and suddenly, your subject's attire is as sharp as your photography skills. Throw a makeup artist into the session, and those minor skin blemishes vanish, not in post-production, but right there in the camera. The result? A headshot that looks polished and professional, making your client shine and, by extension, making your portfolio shine even brighter.

But let's take this beyond the studio lights and into the heart of your local community. Engaging with your community might sound daunting, but it's about connecting with the world outside your door. Participate in local events, offer to shoot at community gatherings, or hold a mini-exhibit at your local café showcasing your work. Each activity increases your visibility and roots you as a vital part of the community fabric. People start recognizing your face, not just your photographs, and in a business where familiarity breeds trust, this can lead to a steady stream of clients who feel a personal connection to you.

Lastly, immerse yourself in photography groups and online forums. Yes, the digital realm is teeming with communities that span the globe. These platforms are about sharing your latest shots and learning, sharing, and growing together. Do you have a lighting dilemma? Throw it into a forum. Chances are someone has been there and figured it out. Want feedback on a new editing technique? Please post it in a group and watch the constructive critiques roll in. These interactions, while virtual, can significantly impact your real-world skills and knowledge. Plus, they keep you on your toes, pushing you to stay current and competitive in an ever-evolving industry.

So there you have it. Networking and collaboration might seem like just another to-do on your ever-growing list, but they are indispensable tools in your photography toolkit. They open doors to new opportunities and learning and enrich your professional journey, making it a shared adventure rather than a solitary slog. So step out, reach out, and watch as your network becomes your net worth in more ways than one.

Staying Creative and Inspired: Continuing Your Photographic Journey

Continuing Education

There's a little secret in the photography world that keeps the best snapping stunning shots, year after year—never stop learning. It's tempting to rest on your laurels once you've mastered the exposure triangle or nailed your post-processing workflow, but let's face it: photography is as dynamic as a flashbulb. Diving into ongoing education is a must to keep your skills as sharp as your lenses. Workshops can open your eyes to new techniques and trends, whether in-person or online. Picture yourself in a workshop learning the latest in lighting technology or a new method of post-editing that might revolutionize your workflow. These learning experiences are skill enhancers and great venues to rub shoulders with peers and mentors who can offer fresh perspectives and insights.

Online courses and tutorials offer a buffet of learning opportunities at your fingertips, often available on-demand to suit your hectic schedule. Platforms like Udemy, Coursera, or even specific photography-focused sites offer courses ranging from the basics to advanced niche-specific skills. But don't just watch—practice. Apply these new skills in simulated setups or shoots to transform theoretical knowledge into practical prowess. And let's not forget the wealth of books and magazines out there. Sometimes, flipping through the pages of a well-crafted photography book can spark that creative flame as effectively as any high-tech workshop.

Personal Projects

Personal projects can be your creative oasis if you feel the creative burnout from all those client headshots. These projects are your playground. They're where you can experiment without constraints, try out bizarre compositions, play with unconventional lighting, or dive into a photography genre you've never tried before. It could be a documentary project on the life of urban street performers or a surreal portrait series inspired by your favorite sci-fi movies. These personal endeavors push the boundaries of your creativity, challenging you to think and shoot outside your comfort zone.

The beauty of personal projects lies in their ability to reignite your passion for photography. They remind you why you picked up a camera in the first place—not just to pay the bills but to capture the world through your unique lens. Plus, these projects can unexpectedly open new doors. Sharing this work on social media or photography exhibitions can attract attention from potential clients who might be drawn to your work's style and emotional depth, leading to new professional opportunities.

Seeking Inspiration

Inspiration fuels creativity; luckily, it's scattered generously throughout the world. For headshot photographers, inspiration can come from a myriad of sources. Art's diverse forms and expressions can spark new ideas for poses, compositions, or themes. Visit galleries or dive into art books and observe how artists use color, light, and form. Cinema, another rich source, offers a visual feast of framing, lighting, and character portrayal that can translate beautifully into portrait photography. Watch films critically, noting how cinematographers compose shots and directors elicit emotions, then bring those cinematic techniques into your photography.

Fashion, too, influences portrait photography profoundly. The play of fabrics, the evolution of styles, and the boldness of runway shows can inspire fresh approaches to how you dress and style your subjects. Follow fashion blogs, watch emerging designers, or even collaborate with a fashion stylist to bring a couture edge to your headshots. And don't overlook the everyday—sometimes, the most powerful inspiration comes from the people and places in your daily life. A smile from a stranger, the atmosphere of a café, or the chaos of a city street could spark the concept for your next big project.

Adapting and Evolving

In a field as dynamic as photography, adaptability is critical. The tools, technologies, and trends are constantly changing, and keeping pace can be the difference between staying relevant and becoming obsolete. Embrace change, whether upgrading to the latest camera gear to enhance image quality or adopting new software to streamline your workflow. But it's not just about gear and gadgets; it's also about adapting your business strategies and marketing efforts to align with changing market conditions and client expectations.

Stay flexible in your business plans, ready to pivot when a particular strategy doesn't pan out or when a new opportunity presents itself. It's shifting more business online in response to global changes or tapping into a new market segment that suddenly shows potential. Keep your ear to the ground, listen to client feedback, and stay attuned to industry trends. This proactive approach ensures that your photography business survives and thrives, no matter what challenges or changes the market throws your way.

As you continue on this exciting photographic journey, remember that staying creative and inspired is not a passive process. It requires action—learning, experimenting, seeking out new sources of inspiration, and being willing to change and evolve. This active pursuit of growth and inspiration will keep your passion for photography vibrant and your career in photography dynamic and fulfilling.

As we wrap up this chapter on staying creatively charged and inspired, remember a photographer's journey is one of constant discovery and re-invention. Each image you capture is not just a reflection of your subject but of your journey as an artist and a professional. As we turn to the next chapter, we'll explore even more ways to refine your craft and expand your horizons in photography. So keep your lenses clean and your mind open—the best is yet to come.

Conclusion

Well, folks, we've finally zoomed our way to the end of this enlightening journey through headshot photography. From mastering the basics in Chapter 1 to diving deep into the sophisticated lighting and post-processing techniques, we've traveled together from the raw novice terrains to the peaks of skilled artistry. Each chapter, a stepping stone, has built upon the last, elevating your skills and confidence shot by shot.

Reflecting on our adventure, it's clear that headshot photography is much more than just snapping pictures. It's about mastering the dance of light and shadows, learning the delicate art of directing and posing to capture the very soul of your subjects, and refining those captures into polished gems through post-processing. And let's remember the grand finale of knitting all these skills into the fabric of a successful photography business.

But here's the kicker—whether you're aiming to become the next big name in photography or just looking to seriously upgrade your Instagram game, the skills and insights we've shared are universal. They don't discriminate based on your fancy equipment or background; they're about your passion and dedication to the craft.

So, what's next on your photographic horizon? I urge you not to let this be the end. The world of photography is as vast as it is dynamic. Keep exploring, keep learning. New techniques, styles, and technologies are popping up faster than you can say "cheese." Experiment fearlessly because every mistake is just a lesson in disguise, and every triumph is a story waiting to be told.

And speaking of stories, remember that your work can do more than fill space on a hard drive. You're capturing moments, personalities, and potential. Each headshot could be the key to someone's dream job or a cherished memory for a family. That's a magical ability, so wield it with pride and care.

I can't send you off without a massive thank you for picking up this book and walking this path with me. Sharing these insights has been as rewarding for you as for me. But our journey doesn't have to end here. I invite you to keep the conversation going—share your work, highs and lows, and victories. Reach out with feedback, or better yet, share your success stories. Let's keep this community thriving, learning from each other and drawing inspiration from every snapshot shared.

So, here's to you and your photography journey—may it be long, fruitful, and filled with the joy of capturing the world, one incredible headshot at a time. Go out there and make every shot count!

Cheers to clicking more than just the shutter; remember, the best is yet to come.

Headshot Photography
Worksheets

Headshot Wardrobe Planning Worksheet

This worksheet is for readers to plan their wardrobe choices for their headshot session. It includes space for notes on color schemes and clothing options and a checklist summarizing various lighting techniques for headshots.

Part 1: Wardrobe Selection

Clothing Options:
- Business Attire (e.g., Suit, Blouse, Tie)
- Casual Wear (e.g., Sweater, Button-down Shirt)
- Creative Attire (e.g., Artsy Outfits, Unique Accessories)
- Special Attire (e.g., Uniforms, Themed Costumes)

Color Schemes:
- Neutrals (e.g., Whites, Blacks, Grays)
- Earth Tones (e.g., Browns, Greens)
- Bold Colors (e.g., Reds, Blues)
- Personal Favorites (Specify: ______________)

Notes on Clothing:
Write down any specific clothing items or styles you want to wear.
Consider the message or mood you want to convey through your outfit.

Headshot Lighting Techniques

Part 2: Lighting Techniques Checklist

Use this list as a reference during your photoshoot to experiment with different lighting techniques:

Soft Lighting: Creates a flattering, even illumination with minimal shadows.

Rembrandt Lighting: Achieves a triangular highlight on one side of the face.

Split Lighting: Divides the face into equal halves, with one side in light and the other in shadow.

Loop Lighting: A small shadow of the nose on the cheek creates a gentle loop shape.

Butterfly Lighting: Casts a small, symmetrical shadow under the nose.

Broad Lighting: Illuminates the larger side of the face, ideal for slimming effects.

Short Lighting: Highlights the smaller side of the face, providing a sense of depth.

Rim or Hair Light: This technique adds a halo-like rim of light behind the subject, separating them from the background.

Remember, your headshot wardrobe and lighting choices should align with your personal brand and the message you want to convey. Use this worksheet as a tool to plan and communicate your preferences effectively during your headshot session.

Note: This worksheet is for planning purposes and can be customized according to individual preferences and specific session details.

Headshot Practice Exercises

Here are five exercises for photographers to practice lighting techniques:

1. Single Light Source Experiment:
   - Set up a single light source, such as a studio strobe or a window with natural light.
   - Place a subject or object in front of the light source.
   - Experiment with the positioning and angle of the light to create different shadows and highlights.
   - Observe how changing the light's distance and angle affects the subject's appearance.
2. Three-Point Lighting Setup:
   - Create a classic three-point lighting setup with key, fill, and backlight sources.
   - Position a subject within this lighting setup.
   - Adjust the intensity and direction of each light source to achieve balanced and dramatic lighting.
   - Practice variations of this setup to understand how it can be used for portraits, product photography, and more.
3. Low-Key and High-Key Photography:
   - For low-key photography, use minimal lighting to create a dark and moody atmosphere.
   - For high-key photography, employ bright, even lighting to achieve a clean and airy look.
   - Experiment with different subjects and scenes for both styles to understand how to control light for mood and effect.
4. Reflectors and Diffusers:
   - Use reflectors and diffusers to modify natural or artificial light.
   - Practice bouncing light onto subjects with reflectors to fill in shadows.
   - Try diffusing harsh light with materials like a white sheet or professional diffusers.
   - Understand how these tools can soften or enhance light for better results.
5. Mixed Lighting Conditions:
   - Challenge yourself by shooting in environments with mixed lighting sources (e.g., indoor and outdoor light).
   - Learn how to balance and harmonize different light temperatures (warm and cool) to create cohesive images.
   - Experiment with white balance settings to achieve desired color tones.

These exercises will help photographers develop their lighting skills, from mastering basic setups to handling complex lighting scenarios. Practice and experimentation are key to becoming proficient in lighting techniques.

Also by Amanda Otis

Capturing Your Journey: A Guide to Crafting a Stunning Photography Portfolio (with Helpful Worksheets and 50 Portfolio Building Exercises)

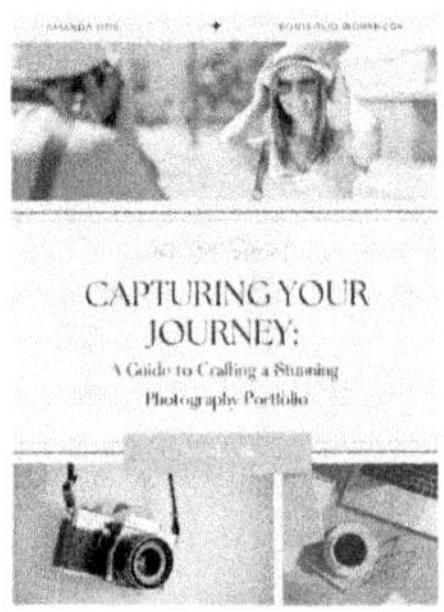

Embark on a transformative journey through the lens with "Capturing Your Journey," a comprehensive guided workbook designed for photographers aspir- ing to build their perfect portfolio. This 26-page workbook is a treasure trove of portfolio-building insights, offering a wealth of information and 50 dynamic exercises tailored to help you curate a portfolio that reflects your unique style and vision.

Discover the art of thematic thinking, find your passion, develop depth in your work, and master the art of tight editing with practical exercises that guide you every step of the way. Whether you're a budding photographer or a seasoned pro, this workbook is your companion in honing your craft and creating a portfolio that stands out.